NICHOLAS *of* CUSA

Erich Meuthen

NICHOLAS
of CUSA

A Sketch for a Biography

Translated from the seventh German edition
with an introduction by David Crowner
and Gerald Christianson

The Catholic University of America Press
Washington, D.C.

© Meuthen, Erich. (1929–)
Originally published in German in 1964
as *Nikolaus von Kues: Skizze einer Biographie*.
This translation was produced from the seventh
edition published in 1992. Overall production,
and all German editions, printed by
Aschendorff Publishing Company,
Münster.
ISBN 3-402-03492-1

Copyright © 2010
The Catholic University of America Press
All rights reserved

Library of Congress Cataloging-in-Publication Data
Meuthen, Erich.
[Nikolaus von Kues, 1401–1464. English]
Nicholas of Cusa : a sketch for a biography /
Erich Meuthen ; translated from the seventh German
edition with an introduction by David Crowner
and Gerald Christianson.
p. cm.
Includes bibliographical references and index.
ISBN 978-0-8132-1787-1 (pbk. : alk. paper)
1. Nicholas, of Cusa, Cardinal, 1401–1464.   I. Title.
BX4705.N58M4713 2010
282.092—dc22   2010014048
[B]

Contents

List of Illustrations

Acknowledgments

To our respect and admiration for Erich Meuthen and his contributions to our knowledge of Nicholas of Cusa and the late Middle Ages we add our deep thanks for his acceptance of our offer to translate a work he modestly called a "sketch." Many friends and colleagues gave us counsel and encouragement along the way. The late H. Lawrence Bond first insisted that it be done. Thomas M. Izbicki, Donald Duclow, and Clyde Lee Miller offered helpful comments and suggestions, as did the participants in the 2006 Gettysburg Conference co-sponsored by the American Cusanus Society and the International Seminar on Late Medieval Theology at Gettysburg Lutheran Seminary, where a session was devoted to Meuthen and the translation. Thanks also go to Morimichi Watanabe for providing this volume with an introductory appreciation of Professor Meuthen. In addition, we are grateful to Dr. Dirk F. Passmann of the Aschendorff Verlag, who kindly granted us permission to translate the work, and to James Kruggel and David McGonagle of the Catholic University of America Press, who, with their advice and instructions, helped guide us on the way toward publication. We are pleased to dedicate our translation to Pat Crowner and Carol Christianson, who have followed our efforts with patience and good humor.

Gettysburg, Pennsylvania
Epiphany, 2010

About This Translation

This book is a translation of the seventh edition of Erich Meuthen's *Nikolaus von Kues: Skizze einer Biographie,* published in 1992 by the Aschendorffsche Verlagsbuchhandlung GmbH & Co., Münster. As translators we faced three interwoven challenges common to the craft: to remain faithful to the original text; to render it in a way that fits the language and culture into which it is being conveyed; and to capture the author's style, tone, and intent.

For the reader's greater ease in following the narrative we have added titles to the sections into which Meuthen divided his text, and we also appended a glossary of terms. At Professor Meuthen's request, Hans Gerhard Senger provided an update of the bibliography of Cusanus research and we are pleased to add it to this volume.

It was with utmost pleasure that we went about our task, and we hope the result is successful enough that readers will hear the voice of Erich Meuthen himself and enjoy and admire his presentation of Nicholas of Cusa.

Erich Meuthen

An Appreciation

MORIMICHI WATANABE

It would be very hard to find someone as qualified as Erich Meuthen to write a biography of Nicholas of Cusa (1401–1464). The following retrospective of Meuthen's remarkable career is offered in appreciation not only for his groundbreaking "sketch" of the fifteenth-century philosopher, theologian, lawyer, reformer, statesman, and cardinal, but in appreciation, in a much broader sense, for Meuthen's outstanding service as scholar and historian.

I was fortunate to have visited Meuthen in Germany on more than one occasion and observed his working methods, as well as the admiring circle of students and colleagues who gathered around him. On one of these visits in 1989 I asked him why there were two separate desks in his library. He told me that one desk was for preparing his university lectures and the other for his Cusanus research—a system I subsequently introduced into my own library. Here was a visible example of his enviable organization and diligence.

꘎

Born in Mönchengladbach, near Cologne, on May 31, 1929, Erich Meuthen studied history, German philology, and philosophy at the University of Cologne. He was attracted to Cusanus research under the influence of Josef Koch (1885–1967), known for his detailed studies of Cusanus's works and their context. Meuthen's research took him to Italian archives and libraries in the 1950s.

Between 1966 and 1971 he served as Director of the City Archives of Aachen where, after completing his *Habilitation* in 1967, he was also active as lecturer at the *Technologische Hochschule*. Then, in 1971, he was called as Professor of History to the University of Bern in Switzerland, and finally from 1976 to 1994 he held the position of Professor of Medieval and Modern History at his alma mater, the University of Cologne.

Meuthen is a corresponding member of the Heidelberg Academy of Letters and Sciences, a member of the Historical Commission of the Bavarian Academy of Letters and Sciences as well as the Rhineland-Westphalian Academy of Letters and Sciences. He has also been a member of the Board of Advisors of the American Cusanus Society since its establishment in 1985.

❧

Meuthen retired on July 7, 1994. The *Festschrift* celebrating this occasion, entitled *Studien zum 15. Jahrhundert. Festschrift für Erich Meuthen* (2 volumes, Munich, 1994), lists eleven books and ninety-four articles that he had published until that date.

The very first book on the list, *Die letzten Jahre des Nikolaus von Kues* (Cologne, 1958), was a product of his research in Italy during the 1950s. Meuthen's treatment of newly discovered sources, which is both detailed and enlightening, pertains to Cusanus's last years from 1458 to 1464 after he left the Tyrol and came to Rome at the invitation of Pope Pius II.

The volume in hand, *Nikolaus von Kues 1401–1464. Skizze einer Biographie* (Münster, 1964), is the next important book on the list, and has been so well received that it has gone through six more editions (1967, 1976, 1980, 1982, 1985, and 1992). In the preface to the third edition of the *Skizze*, Meuthen noted that revisions were required by the appearance of his *Acta Cusana*, a monumental work that included many new sources and was foreshadowed by the archival research behind his first book. In the foreword to volume I, part l, published in Hamburg in 1976, Meuthen explained that the *Acta Cusana* was to complement published collections of Cusanus's works, such as *Opera omnia* and *Sermones,* by compiling all existing documents, letters, contracts, and other records related to Cusanus and his activities, together with numerous critical comments and annotations. The three parts of the *Acta* would cover his early years, from 1401 to 1452; his middle years, from April 1452 to April 1460; and his final years, from May 1460 to August 1464.

Altogether, thanks to Meuthen's great industry, five volumes have appeared thus far, and constitute a remarkably comprehensive treatment of the man. I know of no other medieval philosopher or theologian whose life, ideas, writings, and activities are so minutely examined.

Of the many other books by Meuthen, one should mention the fundamental study of Cusanus's early career, *Das Trierer Schisma von 1430 auf dem Basler Konzil* (Münster, 1964), during which period—on the eve of the Council of Basel (1431–1449)—Cusanus established his reputation as a negotiator, diplomat, and canon lawyer. Meuthen did not give attention to Cusanus alone, but used this research as a foundation for his contribution to the wider context of Cusanus's century: *Das 15. Jahrhundert* (Munich, 1980; 3rd rev. ed., Munich, 1996).

❧

When one begins to assess Meuthen's work as historian and Cusanus scholar, two points immediately stand out. First, as I mentioned at his retirement some years ago—and the point bears repeating—Meuthen's work is always solidly based on primary sources, some of which were unknown until he discovered them. Second, in addition to Meuthen's emphasis on historical evidence, his command of the secondary literature is truly impressive, including publications from this side of the Atlantic where late medieval and Renaissance studies have made great strides since World War II.

Cusanus scholars respect and admire the pioneering work on Cusanus by the French scholar Edmond Vansteenberghe (1881–1943), but Meuthen has significantly enlarged and deepened the field. Nevertheless, much remains to be done and younger scholars will need to take up the task. I hope that this long-overdue English translation of Meuthen's famous biography will contribute to the growing interest in the man from Kues.

The World of Cusanus,
1401–1464

This book traces the life and ideas of the pivotal fifteenth-century churchman, Nicholas of Cusa (1401–1464). Born just after the new century dawned, Cusanus figured prominently in the intellectual and political crosscurrents of its first fifty years and more. The following introduction seeks to highlight features of Cusanus's age that readers will encounter in the multifaceted career of a man who often stood above the ordinary: a canon lawyer and statesman, a theologian and philosopher, a reformer and mystical writer, a cardinal and confidant of popes. Even when he appears most clearly as a product of his age, he illuminates its shape and character.

The Socio-Political Landscape

The socio-political landscape of Cusanus's day was noted for its contrasts and contradictions. This was the age of Renaissance, the rebirth of humanism, the invention of printing, and voyages of discovery, yet it was also the age of incessant warfare, the invention of gunpowder, urban revolt, prolonged schism, and lingering plague.

At the time Cusanus was born, Europe was still recovering from the devastations of the Black Death, the most virulent of medieval plagues. In a short period, from 1347 to 1350, it had swept from Sicily to Scandinavia. Some estimates claim that a staggering one-third of Europe's population died. Recurrences persisted into the fifteenth century, with an outbreak in 1405.

The terror of the Black Death appears to have had profound

effects on religion and the arts. One view held that "God, for the sins of men, has struck the world with this great punishment of sudden death." In response, some sought a more intense, personal relationship with God, and themes of grief and death persisted.

Medieval society rebounded, however, and Cusanus's century witnessed a rapid growth in population, cities, and commerce. The need for money and the rise of urban centers, a result of increased trade, stimulated the continued expansion of a merchant class that had its own needs and demands, including education and favorable markets. Some merchants—Cusanus's father is an example—found opportunity to increase their earnings by wise investments in property and by judicious loans, sometimes even to cash-strapped aristocrats. While kings and princes sought new ways to raise revenue—usually in the form of taxes—in support of their territorial ambitions, others in the lower strata of society resorted to revolt to redress their grievances.

Some of these same kings and princes stood in the forefront of the developing monarchical states (also referred to as nation states) that emerged from feudal economies. An important consequence was that states challenged the power and prestige of papacy and empire. First, however, the monarchs needed to solve difficult issues such as income and defense. These challenges were intensified in France and England by the Hundred Years War (1337–1453), while a decisive stage was reached in Spain with the marriage of Ferdinand and Isabella (1469).

The situation in Germany, heart of the Holy Roman Empire, was complex and tended to follow a local and regional course. Success at solidifying the empire depended on the energy and resolve of the emperors and their relationship to the territorial princes. Sigismund of Luxembourg became a key figure in the Council of Constance and the ending of the Great Schism, thus adding to the prestige of the empire while, in contrast, the long-reigning but less effective Frederick III of Hapsburg did more to establish his line of succession.

Italy, too, resisted more than regional centralization, especially after the papacy regained control of the Papal States, a territory that cut a swath across the peninsula. While this prevented unification on a larger scale, it did not prevent adventurous cities, powerful princes and *condottieri* from seeking to expand their control. All these emerging sovereignties, from Italy to England, were quick to find authors willing to support royal over papal authority—Marsilius of Padua and John Wyclif among them.

Religious Practices

Across the Holy Roman Empire monasticism continued to play a major role. Since the time of Benedict monks had gathered into monasteries that followed rules for living in community. Over time, some of these affiliated with one another, forming an order. Two of the largest were the Benedictines and the Cistercians who followed the *Rule of St. Benedict*. Regular canons, notably the Augustinians and Premonstratentians, straddled the boundary between monks and secular clergy. The best known of this type were the mendicant orders—Franciscans and Dominicans—who emphasized preaching and teaching among lay folk. Common to all were vows of poverty, chastity, and obedience. When laxity in observance of these vows arose, reformers encouraged stiffer regulations and visitations by an outsider such as a bishop, though these were often met with determined resistance.

A novel source of religious renewal came from a strand of piety called the Modern Devotion (*devotio moderna*). Unlike monastic orders, members of the Devotion did not take the three formal vows even though they retained a high regard for them and lived together in community. The Devotion attracted large numbers of lay men and women, especially from the Netherlands and Rhineland, who wanted to observe a simple piety and a commitment to the poor. The interest of many of these men and women in reliable texts had much in common with the humanists. Despite the association of later scholars such as Erasmus with the Devotion, its influence on fifteenth century education is still debated.

The popularity of the mendicant orders indicates that preaching in the vernacular was more common in Cusanus's time than is often thought. The Franciscan Bernardino of Siena and the Dominican Savonarola became widely known for their dramatic revival sermons in public places, but many lesser-known figures could draw a crowd as well, often to the consternation of local parish priests and their bishops. Although he was a chaplain and not a monk, John Hus attracted a large and dedicated audience to his preaching at the Bethlehem Chapel in Prague. His sermons on reform gained favor with the Bohemian court, but not with Rome.

Still, the focal point of worship within the church itself was the sacrifice of the Mass and the miraculous transformation of bread and wine into the body and blood of Christ. An intensified concern about one's welfare after death led individuals and corporate groups such as guilds to establish endowments that would accumulate prayers for the souls of the departed. These endowments stimulated a rapid expansion of chantries, perpetual masses, and charitable foundations. The intense concern of the faithful also led to greater veneration of the host both within the Mass and in Corpus Christi processions outside, as well as to a fascination with miracles related to the Eucharist, such as bleeding hosts, and to pilgrimages to the sites of these miracles.

Meanwhile, the penitential system remained a central feature of church discipline, and the pious were required to receive communion at least once a year preceded by confession. While the sacrament of penance was based on the remission of sins, expiation was not expected to be completed until after death in purgatory.

Increasingly the church claimed that the papacy presided over a treasury of merits that Christ and the saints had provided from the excess of their good deeds. This treasury allowed the popes to offer indulgences, at first to remit certain punishments in exchange for joining a crusade, but one could also receive a Jubilee Indulgence for making a pilgrimage to Rome to celebrate the turn of the century. However, financial constraints, which frequently plagued the papacy like other territorial monarchies, prompted the Holy See to declare Jubilees with greater frequency, and to turn the sale of indulgences into a lucrative practice.

Astrology

Astrology, especially a fascination with what might be called a mysticism of numbers, flourished in Cusanus's time, even among intellectuals. Numerous councils as far back as the Council of Nicea I (325) had condemned early forms of astrology associated with paganism—Constantine II (316–340) swore to have astrologers ripped apart with iron claws—but by the twelfth century it had regained a prominent role in public life. Virtually every figure of importance, including popes, made use of it. Kings and emperors kept court astrologers and decorated books of divination with tables providing answers to questions such as the appropriate time to marry or wage war. Chairs of astrology were established at universities from Oxford to Vienna.

While such practices, from chantries and bleeding hosts to astrology, may not appeal to modern tastes, these and others like them appeared to many at the time as signs of spiritual vitality rather than a decline in piety and morals. While some decried the abuse of these practices and the penitential system with its sometimes blatant sale of indulgences, others thought that the church had developed a vibrant tradition that met their desires for an effective and meaningful spirituality.

xxi

Renaissance and Humanism

For numerous observers, the most dramatic renewal in the fifteenth century was the Renaissance, the "rebirth" of art and literature. Like the resurgence of mysticism in the Rhineland, exemplified by Meister Eckhart, the Renaissance arose in the midst of the traditional schools of the day—Aristotelian scholasticism, a legacy of the Dominicans Albertus Magnus and Thomas Aquinas, and the newer Nominalism of the Franciscan William of Ockham. Inspired by classical models, the Renaissance began as a literary-rhetorical movement in late fourteenth-century Italy with the poet Petrarch who took Cicero as his guide. The movement spread into Germany in the following century.

The characteristic humanism of the Renaissance involved the *studia humanitatis,* studies such as grammar and rhetoric that were meant to form a free citizen. Humanists had a passion for elegant letter-writing and eloquent discourse and, while they may have espoused no particular system of philosophy or theology, they were generally concerned with immortality, unity, and human dignity.

Even those who were not humanists in the strict sense were indebted to new translations of ancient works. Furthermore, conflicts between Aristotelian scholasticism and the Platonism favored by many humanists stimulated a creative ferment in which some attempted to strike a balance or overcome the dichotomy with fresh perspectives or new presuppositions. The introduction of printed pamphlets and books meant that a curious, and in some sectors more literate, population became increasingly well informed about these developments and their implications for theology and politics.

Most humanists remained committed to the Christian faith, especially as it was represented in early Christian literature, the study of which was enhanced by the discovery of old manuscripts. These studies also helped to increase a sense of historical distance and an awareness of the discontinuity between the early church and what many saw as its current, less worthy, manifestation—a contrast that carried a potential for conflict with the papacy.

The Great Schism and the Councils

Even greater conflict arose from the most devastating event in the fifteenth-century church, and its greatest constitutional crisis, the Great Schism. Division began in 1378 with the election of two popes and continued for nearly forty years. In an attempt to end the schism between one contender in Rome (Gregory XII) and another in Avignon (Benedict XIII), a group of cardinals called the Council of Pisa in 1409, but this merely added another pope (Alexander V). Not until the Council of Constance (1414–1418) did the scandal finally end with the intervention of King Sigismund and the election of Martin V (1417–1431).

Constance also enacted a kind of declaration of conciliar rights in two memorable decrees. *Haec sancta* declared that a council derives its authority directly from Christ and all, even a pope, must obey in matters of faith. *Frequens* provided for the regular assembling of councils, eventually every ten years. Yet while Martin recovered the Papal States and reestablished the papacy's temporal authority, he resisted reform and hesitated to call another council. Finally, on the last day of his life Martin summoned an assembly to meet at Basel (1431–1449). Its convocation was postponed, however, while the papal legate and president, Cardinal Giuliano Cesarini, led a crusade against the Hussites in Bohemia, and nearly lost his life in the ensuing disaster.

The Hussites

The Hussite conflict (1420–1436) had been touched off when Constance tried John Hus and burned him at the stake despite Sigismund's promise of safe conduct. In retaliation, Hus's followers stated their demands in a document known as the Four Articles. These included the free preaching of the Gospel and the distribution of both wine and bread to the laity in communion. Unlike many earlier resistance movements, the Hussites could back their demands with force because they became skillful warriors and tacticians, resisting one crusade after another and even threatening Catholic cities outside of Bohemia.

When the Council of Basel finally opened in September 1431, Cesarini and the members decided to change tactics. They invited a delegation of Hussites to discuss the Four Articles in open sessions. Surprisingly, the Hussites agreed, but the new pope, Eugenius IV, objected. The council pressed forward in violation of his wishes, even threatening to summon him for his recalcitrance. The assembly eventually proposed that the Bohemian church be allowed to practice utraquism (the name given to communion in both kinds) in exchange for returning to the Catholic fold, but when the Hussite delegation took the proposal back to Prague for approval, the movement split apart and the factions went to war.

Not only did Eugenius object to the Hussite negotiations, he attempted to transfer or dissolve the council itself, touching off a lengthy and bitter battle between the two sides over a new and untested question: how should a legitimate council relate to an uncontested pope when the church was no longer mired in schism? Several of the best minds of the day, including Nicholas of Cusa, entered the debate.

Despite these efforts, the conflict continued for nearly two decades during which the church experienced a new schism when Basel deposed Eugenius and elected a layman as Felix V. Since the empire declared itself neutral, the papacy expended considerable energy to defeat Basel and its "anti-pope," especially by assigning articulate ambassadors, such as Cusanus, who could argue the papal case at imperial Diets and conferences.

Islam

The growing crisis in Constantinople provided the popes with an opportunity to tip the balance in their favor. On the outskirts of Western Europe, the forces of Islam were no longer a nuisance; they were a menace. Where once it was an obstacle standing in the way of pilgrims to the Holy Land, the rise to dominance of the Ottoman Turks changed a distant enemy into an increasingly immediate threat, one that pressed ever closer to the Holy Roman Empire.

Appeals for help from the East against the ever-tightening Turkish noose around the Greek capital increased until Pope Eugenius IV invited Eastern and Latin churches to meet together at the Council of Ferrara-Florence (1438–1447) and hammer out an agreement. Still it was not enough to unite the churches. The East rejected the union decree. Nor was it enough to save Constantinople. In a historic blow to Christendom the capital fell to the Turks in 1453, bringing to an end the political independence of the Byzantine Empire that had lasted for over a thousand years. In a short period the Turks advanced to the very gates of Belgrade.

A crusade in defense of Christendom, however, proved more difficult to mount than ever before. The nation states had little to gain. Nevertheless, the crusading ideal remained alive and was revived during the papacy of Pius II, the former humanist Aeneas Sylvius Piccolomini. When too few crusaders responded to his call for a great armada to assemble at Ancona in 1464, the project evaporated as the old pope breathed his last.

Last Act of Friendship

In the act of coming to the aid of Pius II and his crusade, Nicholas of Cusa, the cardinal and longtime confidant of the pope, died three days before him on the road to Ancona. It was August 11.

By then Cusanus had succeeded in participating in, if not actually shaping, nearly every major issue of the more than half-century that life had given him. In addition to his career as an energetic churchman, he also found time to leave a remarkable intellectual legacy that fascinates an unusually broad range of people to this day, from astronomers and mathematicians to church historians, from political theorists to theologians and philosophers.

NICHOLAS *of* CUSA

PREFACE *to the*
SEVENTH EDITION

As was true for the third edition of this book, the text has undergone a thorough review for this seventh edition, the most noticeable changes being various additions that, as before, have been prompted by the ongoing, lively Cusanus research. Indeed, much more ought to have been added, but I did not want to jeopardize the sketchlike character that was the concept behind the first version of 1964. For this reason I avoided expanding the text too much with more biographical details.

I was able to leave the foreword of 1964 as written, and properly so. It belongs to an undertaking that, as its reception shows, has needed no substantial alteration, and it is doubtful that changes would have been useful in any case.

The *Acta Cusana,* first announced in the preface to the third edition, keeps growing and forms the documentary basis for this edition of the *Sketch* as well. The third installment that will present the 1451–1452 legation to Germany is in the offing. Indeed, as has become evident during its preparation, the wealth of material is even more extensive than had been anticipated. Readers of this *Sketch* should pick up the *Acta* now and then in order to hear the voice of Cusanus much more directly than is possible in this little book. Essentially the *Sketch* can serve only as an approach to Cusanus, and readers will no doubt agree that to expect anything more is unrealistic.

E.M., Cologne, 1992

I

FOREWORD

To outline the life of Cusanus with a "sketch" seems to be taking an inordinate risk. The highly regarded biography that the Frenchman, Edmond Vansteenberghe, devoted to the man from the Mosel will soon be half a century old. While an immense amount of source information was already at his disposal, since then the mountain of biographical material has piled up to over five thousand documents. The wealth of Cusanus studies—contributions from the most diverse academic disciplines aimed at understanding this unique man—is overwhelming. On the other hand, people are justified in wishing to be introduced, at least in brief, to Cusanus's eventful life as it presents itself in the information we currently have. This little book desires simply to respond to such a wish.

This sketch probably would not have come into being without the persuasive and optimistic encouragement of the Academic Council of the Cusanus Society that brings together leading Cusanus scholars. At its meeting on September 21, 1963, it urged the author to write this sketch for the five hundredth anniversary of Nicholas of Cusa's death. Without completely rounding things out, and leaving out detailed documentation, the part must stand for the whole if the sketch is to serve as a resumé. It does not present itself as a definitive biography, but only as a kind of preview.

The *Sketch* intends primarily to discover the man and to understand his work only in regard to himself, without developing it fully. As a result, the book must abbreviate many things and pass over even more in order to stay within the limits set for it. It can only trace an outline. Instead of coloring in the defined space, as we would much desire, the *Sketch* can offer only sparing colors along the edge. Even so, seemingly peripheral matters often begged for space. They did this not because they regarded themselves as particularly important, but because they believed that in the light they shed they were representative of broader insights, and because they knew, given their subject, which things that came into view warranted inclusion.

Furthermore, I have tried to assign weight to the individual stages in Cusanus's life somewhat differently than the varying amounts of material for the respective stages would suggest. Whereas we follow the period of growth and development of Cusanus's character with great attentiveness, we must be satisfied with many a summary about the maturation and development in the second half of his life.

In being consistent with the character of the book as a concise introduction and guide the author must forego footnotes. So, too, in the no less sparing brevity of these prefatory lines the author wishes to "abridge" the obligation to acknowledge all those who are laboring on Nicholas of Cusa. I would have to praise so many! Nevertheless, in this closing note I wish to fulfill a deeply felt duty by expressing special thanks and admiration to the Nestor of Cusanus research, Josef Koch, whom I have the privilege of calling my teacher.

A SKETCH
for a BIOGRAPHY

Birth and Name

He was born in 1401. This we ascertain from the inscription on his grave, and the year is confirmed by other references. His birthplace gave him the name under which he entered history. In 1430 he referred to himself for the last time using his family name: Nicolaus Cancer—in German, Krebs. Cryfftz, Krieffts, Kreves, and similar variations indicate the Mosel-Franconian dialect. As early as his first university registration in 1416 he added his birthplace: Nycolaus Cancer de Coeße. In his German correspondence he usually wrote Niclas von Cuße. He Latinized the name to Nicolaus de Cußa or also Cusa—forms of the day that were typical for his village on the Mosel.

In 1440 Aeneas Sylvius named him Nicolaus Cusanus for the first time. Prior to this the Italian humanists called him Nicolaus Treverensis. He had given himself this scholarly name as a young man. While this name is not seen after 1435, the name "Krebs" continued to be used for the rest of his life, above all by his political opponents. One senses the malicious disparagement it implies, beginning with the attacks of his opponents at the Council of Basel and continuing on to the *Invective* of 1461 that Gregor Heimburg, no doubt Nicholas's most bitter enemy, opens with the words "Cancer Cusa Nycolae!"

Nicholas himself kept a visual representation of his name on his coat of arms. It shows a red crab on a gold field. It is probably the family coat of arms since his brothers and sisters used it as well. On his oldest seal a moon and a star accompany the crab. Entirely a child of his time, Nicholas believed in the influence of the stars. He possessed an astrological treatise in which marginal notes specifically highlight the sentences that place the year 1433, when his own star began its meteoric rise, under the auspicious sign of the crab. By 1425 he had already composed an astrologically interpreted history of the world covering the time up to Emperor Gallienus.

Family Background

Nicholas's parents were Johan Cryfftz, who was called Cryfftz Henne, and his wife Katharina, daughter of Hermann Roemer. In 1408 and 1414 the Bernkastel **magistrate**, Clais Roemer, officially registered land purchases made by the Cryfftz couple involving annual payments.[1] Perhaps Nicholas received his first name from Clais—a shortened version of Nicholas. In 1431 the magistrates Claes and Peter Roemer are named together. Another native of Bernkastel, Casper Romer, who died in Aachen in 1451 as the **canon** of Münstermaifeld and St. Mary's, is specifically identified as a blood relative of Cusanus. Johannes Romer called himself Cusanus's *"nepot,"* nephew. Romer, born around 1425, came from Briedel, down the Mosel River near Zell. After the death of Cardinal Cusanus, Romer was director of the St. Nicholas Hospital in Kues for a short time. Matthias Römer from Graach, who in 1493 relinquished inheritance claims on the Krebs house in Kues, must also have been a close relative.

Among the younger nephews of Cusanus, Simon von Wehlen gained special recognition. Cusanus named him **vicar-general** of Brixen. Simon von Wehlen's uncle on his mother's side was Simon

---

1. Editor's note: Terms in bold are listed in the Glossary.

Kolb, also called Simon of Kues, who was at first assistant director of the hospital under Johannes Römer, and then from 1466 until his death in 1467 director. How Cusanus's mother was related to the individual members of the Römer family is still uncertain. Her father was already dead by 1401. She herself died in 1427.

We know that Cusanus had two sisters and one brother. Margareta, the older sister who was married to a magistrate in Trier, died early, certainly before 1447. She, like her younger sister, Klara, left no children. Klara's first marriage was to a Trier citizen, Johann Plynisch; her second, after 1441, was to the Trier magistrate, Paul von Bristge, who served repeatedly as mayor. He came from a patrician family in Trier. His father, Clais von Bristge, was also a magistrate in Trier.

Klara's will, which she drew up in 1473, the year of her death, immediately after the passing of her husband, testifies to her affluence. In accordance with her wish, she was laid to rest in front of the altar in the hospital chapel. Today one finds her gravestone bearing her expressive face—probably the work of a Trier stone-carver—set in the south wall of the chapel (see figure 1). A gentle smile passes over her serene features. In his later years Theodor Heuss confessed his secret, young love for the image of this graceful woman. The memorial book of the hospital in Kues intimates that she was a self-assured patrician.

Johannes, the somewhat younger brother, does not stand out because of any accomplishment that comes even close to resembling the greatness of Cusanus. He was ordained a priest at the end of the 1420s, a decade before his brother. Our knowledge about him is limited for the most part to his **benefices** that he more or less owed to his brother. He was a member of the **collegiate chapters** of St. Simeon in Trier, St. Peter Outside the Walls in Mainz, and St. Mary's in Aachen. He became **provost** of Innichen in the Tyrol and received income from the office of provost in Oldenzaal in the

FIGURE I. Klara Kriftz, sister of Cusanus, as portrayed on her gravestone in the chapel of St. Nicholas Hospital, Kues.

FIGURE 2. Cusanus and his brother, Johannes. Detail from the triptych above the altar in the chapel of St. Nicholas Hospital, Kues.

Netherlands. In 1450 his brother had the pope transfer the parish church of Bernkastel to him, where he already had been assigned the income from an **endowed altar** for several years.

The fact that Nicholas entrusted Johannes, as his closest relative, to oversee the construction of the hospital does not say much, since Johannes had very competent people at his side. Nicholas and Johannes became sole and equal inheritors of their father's estate after coming to an agreement with their sister and brother-in-law on an appropriate pension for the couple. Hence, the brothers became cofounders of the hospital. Johannes died in 1456 and was buried in the parish church of Bernkastel. In the painting above the chapel altar (see figure 2), it is Johannes—certainly not Cusanus's secretary, Peter of Erkelenz, as has been supposed—who is kneeling behind his brother at the foot of the cross in the pose of a founder. The painting is no doubt by the supposed Dutch "Master of Mary's Life."

Family Status and Nicholas's Youth

Our consideration of Cusanus's relatives has turned our attention to respected circles of society, so it is no surprise that Cusanus's father was a member of these circles, too. He was counted among the dignitaries of Kues and was a circuit judge. In 1435 he was mentioned by name as one of forty-three prominent personages of the electorate of Trier who were on the side of Ulrich of Manderscheid in the contention between the two rivals, Manderscheid and Raban of Helmstadt, for the office of archbishop.

In 1428 a Mathias Cancer de Cusa was canon in Pfalzel and at St. Simeon in Trier. After Mathias's death Cusanus's brother succeeded him as canon in 1430. In 1415 the son-in-law of a Hencken Crifftz is named in a purchase on credit by Henne and Katherina Crifftz. In 1466 property in Trier belonging to Krieffcz Henczen, a boatman, is mentioned. The occupation of this boatman directs our attention back to Cusanus's father.

Henne Krebs was also a boatman, and thus a merchant. His imposing house stood directly on the banks of the Mosel. He had expanded it in 1401, or shortly before, through the purchase of the neighboring house. This was not his only acquisition. Henne Krebs bought numerous annuity and income producing properties in succeeding years, mostly in Kues and Bernkastel, but also in surrounding villages. Over time the holdings increased in size, and landed gentry of Trier became his debtors. In 1412 the Governor of

Hunolstein, by mortgaging the village of Gonzerath, sold Krebs his **tithe** there, and in 1419 transferred to him the income from the governorship of Kues. In 1445 Knight Wilhelm of Esch sold him an income producing property at Bekond near Trier. In 1447 Johann, the younger governor of Hunolstein, who had already taken over from his father, turned over to Cusanus's father, along with numerous income producing properties, his entire vineyard acreage in the regions of Bernkastel and Graach.

Throughout his life Nicholas of Cusa proved to be a skillful, shrewd, and thrifty businessman. His open attitude toward money, business, and profit did not escape the sharp reproach that this was incompatible with being a member of the clergy. However, this reproach missed the mark in terms of pomp and luxury since Nicholas was unpretentious and led a simple life. He remained constantly active, engaged in matters both large and small. The distinctive business mentality he inherited shows through everywhere in his life.

From early on Nicholas was closely associated with the aristocratic Manderscheid family. In 1457 this family was raised to the rank of imperial counts, and through inheritance of the houses of Schleiden and Blankenheim it enjoyed preeminence among the nobility in the Eifel region for several decades. We do not know when or why Nicholas's association with the family began, but it seems likely that his father's connections with the nobility at least paved the way.

To a great extent we are still in the dark about Cusanus's early years. His name does not appear until his registration at the University of Heidelberg in 1416. Then, in the fashion of later centuries, legend filled in where the historical record failed. Legend tells of a rift between father and son. According to this story the son's brooding nature destroyed the father's hopes of seeing the family and his career live on in Nicholas. Historical sources know only of the two getting along well together, leaving the novelistic appeal to the realm of fiction.

Influence of the *Devotio Moderna*

Legend also has Nicholas attending school at Deventer and living in the house of the **Brethren of the Common Life**, even though we are unable to say where he first went to school. Not until the middle of the seventeenth century did the local historical record of Deventer draw the conclusion that Nicholas had attended school there. This conclusion was probably reached because of the *Bursa Cusana*, the student hostel set up with funds from Cusanus's estate. Yet in his will Nicholas identified no particular place for the hostel other than it ought to be located in "Northern Germany." Not until later, on the advice of those who conducted a hospital inspection—the Carthusian **prior** of Koblenz and the Augustinian canon-prior of Niederwerth—was Deventer chosen for the hostel. Probably the prior of Niederwerth directed attention to Deventer as the site for the hostel since his cloister was a part of the **Windesheim Congregation** and associated with the cloistered sisters of communities of the Brethren of the Common Life. They lived in the spirit of piety called at that time *devotio moderna*, **"Modern Devotion."**

The first contact of which we are certain between Cusanus and the Windesheim Congregation was by way of Niederwerth at the beginning of the 1430s. Nicholas was a friend of Peter Eller, chaplain of the archbishop of Trier, whom Nicholas succeeded in the **deanery** of Oberwesel in 1427 when Eller entered the Augustinian monastery in Neuss. Soon Nicholas arranged that those Windesheim individuals who had been driven out of Zwolle could find refuge at the cloister in Niederwerth. When, in the turmoil surrounding the bishopric of Trier in 1435, the **foundation** was again called into question, Cardinal **Legate** Cesarini appointed Nicholas of Cusa administrator of the cloister. The high regard Cusanus had for the Windesheim sisters is reflected in his specific reference to the rule in Niederwerth, when in 1451 he commended the Windesheim Congregation to the **mendicant orders** in Trier as a model.

Other circumstances lead us to presume that Nicholas did not attend school in Deventer. For example, in 1451 the town of Oldenzaal, located in the same province as Deventer, was proposed as a place for negotiations to resolve the feud over who was to become bishop of Münster. Nicholas, who had expended a great deal of energy trying to settle the dispute, declared that he could say nothing about the choice of Oldenzaal since he was unacquainted with the nature of the territory. Another circumstance is that Johannes Busch, chronicler of the Windesheim order, welcomed the visit that Cusanus paid to Dutch cloisters, above all to Windesheim itself, during his legation journey of 1451. Busch wished fervently to meet the person about whose virtue he had heard so much. Would not Cusanus's visit to Deventer have resulted in a moving reunion celebration? Yet contemporary sources report the opposite. The brothers approached the legate, who was staying at the court of the bishop of Utrecht, with great apprehension. They hoped he would not believe the charges that had been brought against them. Neither of these circumstances indicates that Nicholas had spent formative years of his youth in Deventer. Nevertheless, people continue to be fascinated with the idea that Nicholas wanted the life of his hospital foundation to be secure forever in the same spirit in which he had grown up.

Cusanus set before the hospital as a model, both in letter and spirit, the community of Augustinians in the cloisters of the Windesheim Congregation. The spirit of the *devotio moderna*, transmitted by the Brethren of the Common Life as well as by the Windesheim communities, began to spread as a movement of religious renewal at the end of the fourteenth century. This movement desired to renew the Christianity of its day, which was becoming increasingly impersonal, containing less and less heartfelt piety. The *devotio moderna* sought to do this by means of a personally experienced, formed, and lived faith at whose center stands the God-man and Savior. Without disparaging education it strove for simplicity and humility in the "imitation of Christ," which was the programmatic title of the movement's main literary work. Special value was placed on reading the Scriptures. Unlike Petrarch, who studied the ancient world in order to see it anew for its own sake, the *devotio moderna* studied it for the sake of the New Testament. Above all, the movement turned against the predominance of the Schools. Scholasticism, once so impressive, destroyed itself in unfruitful squabbles. Its method of questioning and disputation became artful frivolity. Knowledge and wisdom were no longer joined.

According to the *devotio moderna,* the opportunity to perceive what is good and true ought to be available to everyone. The aim of the new program, based on the certainty that intimate unity with God bestows on each person the foundation of genuine wisdom, was education of the simple believer, of the "layperson." The movement developed a lifestyle that it perceived to be in the mystical tradition of a Bonaventure, with a favorite work being the *Mystical Theology* of Jean Gerson.

We know that among the earliest books in Nicholas of Cusa's possession were Bonaventure's *Journey of the Mind to God* (*Itinerarium mentis in Deum*) and Gerson's *Mystical Theology*. Although we can date his acquisition of them tentatively only to his early years, the books do indicate that his acquaintance with the body of thought of the *devotio moderna* reaches far back in his life. Running through his works in manifold variations are the themes of education of the laity, the hunt for wisdom, the God-man and Savior, and the vision of God. He leaves behind the scholastic method of disputation, letting his thoughts unfold in conversation in an organic manner. When and where he found his way into this world we still do not know. Perhaps it was not until the second half of the 1420s, a period whose significance for his intellectual development is becoming more and more clear.

Heidelberg and Padua

In Heidelberg Nicholas, the student of the seven liberal arts, became acquainted with academic study. It was dominated by the Nominalism of the *via moderna* that Marsilius of Inghen had introduced in Heidelberg twenty years earlier. We know nothing about the significance of the one-year stay for the young Cusanus. Twenty-five years later in a controversy with Nicholas, the Heidelberg Professor Johannes Wenck disparagingly gave him the lowest academic title, Bachelor of Liberal Arts. It is uncertain whether he left Heidelberg in 1417 with this degree.

Nicholas turned to Padua for the study of **canon law**. He finished in 1423 with the degree of Doctor of Canon Law that entitled him to give lectures on the canons. It is certain that one of his teachers was Prosdocimus de Comitibus, not an original thinker, but an industrious and skillful compiler. Nicholas attended his lectures on ecclesiastical procedural law, and we still have his notes on these lectures from 1423. His numerous glosses in them lead us to surmise that he also used them later in his own practice of procedural law. The close relationship to his teacher is made clear in one of these marginal notes that names Prosdocimus his "master and extraordinary father." With these words he certainly is expressing something more personal than he did in his oft-cited dedication of *On Learned Ignorance* (*De docta ignorantia*) to "his most esteemed teacher," Cardinal Cesarini. The most recent archival discoveries of Paolo Sambin have revealed that Nicholas lived in the house of Prosdocimus while in Padua.

It was not until Nicholas was at Padua that Cesarini, who was not much older than Nicholas, received his Doctorate in Secular and Canon Law at the same university. Cesarini probably also lectured after that. He left Padua at the latest in 1421. One of his pupils was the gifted Capranica, born in 1400. As early as 1426, he and his teacher were elevated to the cardinalate. Until his death in 1458 Capranica was closely connected to Nicholas. In 1427 Capranica broke out in tears when he learned about Sigismund of Tyrol's threat against his friend. So it is that in Padua Cusanus made important connections for the first time with personages who soon had rank and influence in the church. With them he was no doubt led beyond professional interests into the urgent ecclesiastical and political questions of his day.

Nicholas faced an epoch of disintegration and fragmentation. In 1417 the Council of Constance put an end to the most unfortunate of all schisms that had culminated in three popes opposing one another. Each excommunicated the others and issued an **interdict** against them and their followers. Wars and feuds battered Europe. The brutalization of medieval society took on ever more cruel forms, and it would not be until after further dreadful centuries that society would gradually submit itself to the insights of more rational thinking.

The social tensions were joined by basic problems of human existence. Famine and epidemics—for example, the plague appeared for the first time in 1348 and repeated itself periodically from then on—shook the western world. They generated an overwhelming desire for salvation. This desire led to psychopathic forms of overexcited religiosity that became entangled with deep superstitions and scarcely perceived the heart of the Christian faith any longer. The piety atomized into innumerable forms of saint worship, private endowments, and other religious practices of a peripheral nature. Altars and chapels were installed around the expansive spaces within the cathedrals.

Increasingly absent was the capacity to synthesize, to grasp the whole and its core. Nominalism challenged the real existence of the universal; the particular stood out more and more sharply. From this Marsilius of Padua and Ockham drew particularistic consequences for church and state, the implementation of which could not help but ask too much of their contemporaries and put societal structures in jeopardy. Cusanus's thought reveals a tension as, on the one hand, he is fascinated and carried along by the movements of his time, while on the other hand, he attempts to defend against their dangers with a synthesis that provides a solution. The mention of Padua naturally awakens immediately the memory of Marsilius, who one hundred years earlier had authored *The Defender of Peace* (*Defensor pacis*). Can we believe Cusanus's admission that he had not become acquainted with the work until he was writing *The Catholic Concordance* (*De concordantia catholica*) in 1433?

We know for certain that in Padua Nicholas entered the circle of pupils of Francesco Zabarella, who was active there from 1394 to 1411. Zabarella, more than other supporters of the conciliar theory before him, emphasized that the agreement, or the consent, of the governed is the prerequisite for legitimate rule in church and state. Thus, he taught that the election of the pope is legitimate only when he is chosen with the consent of the whole body of believers as represented by the council fathers—bishops and prelates—whom the believers have elected. The College of Cardinals is to be the standing representative body of the church, and only if the pope and cardinals were to disagree would the council, as a more broadly representative body, take their place. Thus, he constructed a hierarchy of representative bodies whose foundation, in every case, is formed by the whole body of believers that merely "unfolds" (Zabarella says, "*explicatur*") in its first servant, the pope.

In his doctrine Zabarella was less an original thinker than a fruitful summarizer of what tradition offered him, from Marsilius and Ockham to Conrad of Gelnhausen, Henry of Langenstein and others. Also included were no less influential contemporaries like Pierre d'Ailly and Dietrich of Niem who developed variations on the tradition. By doing this Zabarella became a culminating point in the history of ideas regarding social theory. Yet it was precisely at this time, fostered by the doctrine of the medieval jurists, that the absolute ruler who was unlimited in power emerged as the figure to shape western history, championing in a fundamentally different way the issues of restructuring state and society in the late Middle Ages.

In quoting Francesco Zabarella's commentary on the decrees several times in his *Catholic Concordance,* Nicholas is no doubt returning to a work with which he had become acquainted in Padua. This work contains Zabarella's *Tract on the Schism* in which Nicholas found a detailed commentary on the proposition that lays the foundation for the doctrine of consent, that is: whatever affects all must be approved by all. Nicholas regarded this proposition as a cornerstone of his own work.

Intellectual Life in Padua

Not only political theory led Nicholas beyond the usual scope of his discipline. In *The Catholic Concordance* he reports in detail about the customary election process in Venice. As a young politician he was no less interested in the political practices of the lordships to whose *terra firma* Padua belonged since 1406. Later, as well, he cannot let go of the question of how best to structure the voting process, since it is in voting that the individual's constitutive decision comes to life at the grass roots level. Consequently, it is no surprise that even in his later reform activity during his German legation of 1451 Nicholas develops original election procedures that one could classify within today's election taxonomy as "graduated voting." Although he is fascinated by number or quantity here he emphatically integrates the qualitative element in order that the "best" person or policy can win.

The Padua of that day was the focal point of intellectual life as Paris had been earlier, and offered in every respect a wealth of educational resources. Not only had Padua's reputation in jurisprudence already surpassed the rank of Bologna, but also disciplines in the liberal arts were attracting attention. Vittorino da Feltre, professor of rhetoric, was developing his famous humanistic-literary school, and Nicholas probably became acquainted with the Florentine humanist at this time. Also of note is Paolo del Pozzo Toscanelli, four years older and a native of Florence, who studied medicine in Padua. Later he became famous as a mathematician and astronomer, influenced Brunelleschi and Leonardo da Vinci, and then inspired none other than Columbus to his voyage of discovery. In Padua Nicholas struck up a lifelong friendship with Toscanelli that was accompanied by scholarly interchange. In 1443 Toscanelli sent him Ambrose Traversari's translation of the *Mystical Theology* by Dionysius the Areopagite. Not many years later Nicholas dedicated his work, *On Geometric Transmutation* (*De transmutationibus geometricis*), to Toscanelli, and in 1457 he had him appear as a conversation partner in *The Squared Circle* (*Quadratura circuli*). Nicholas visited him several times in Florence. When Cusanus had his first life-threatening illness in 1461 Toscanelli hurried to his bedside in Rome, and in 1464 Toscanelli, as doctor and friend, was at the side of his dying companion.

In 1422 Prosdocimus de Beldomandis was appointed to the new academic chair in music and astrology in Padua. At that time astronomy and astrology were mingled together. Even Kepler was simultaneously astronomer and astrologist. Did Cusanus attend lectures by Beldomandi? Cusanus's interest in everything that had to do with numbers, arithmetic, geometry, and quantitative relationships of every sort was far more than an intellectual diversion.

The symbols of numbers and figures dominate his speculation every step of the way.

The universal breadth of Padua's intellectual life suited Cusanus's interest in a comprehensive education. Perhaps Venice also offered him his first knowledge of Greek—Vittorino da Feltre spoke it—and thereby opened an entirely new horizon that allowed him to look out beyond the borders of western wisdom and culture.

An experience of an entirely different sort was listening to the sermons that Bernardino of Siena was preaching in Padua at that time. Cusanus heard him again in Rome in 1424. The powerfully eloquent Franciscan had gone to Rome in response to the pope's wish that he come and rouse the people to remorse and repentance. Cusanus, in one of his own sermons of 1457, recalls the words of the saint: "The preacher who has fire in his soul can ignite a fire with dead coals." Bernardino's Latin sermon notes that have come down to us are, admittedly, dry and difficult to work with. They are more like theological treatises, and are only skeletal outlines. However, a cloth-shearer from Siena has handed the sermons down to us in precise detail just as the saint preached them before the people, and in these transcriptions the sermons reveal their compelling pastoral power. In the summer of 1450, eight weeks after the canonization of Bernardino, Nicholas dedicated a chapel in Fontecolombo, a Franciscan convent near Rieti, not only in honor of the order's founder, but also in honor of Saint Bernardino and of Saint Wendelin, patron saint of his parish in his homeland.

Nicholas of Cusa left behind an imposing production of almost 300 sermons. Delving deeply into the mysteries of the Christian faith, they revolve around the theme of the divine-human redeemer. Nicholas wrote them down in the form of condensed Latin notes from which he preached. Reminiscent of Bernardino's outlines, the sermon notes scarcely give us a sense of the great impact that Nicholas's actual preaching in the vernacular had on his listeners. The records of Bernardino's sermons give us insight into the relationship between the plans on paper and the performance in the pulpit. In comparison, the sermons of Cusanus rise again and again to an intellectual niveau that causes us to doubt now and then whether, even if he expressed things in a different way, his listeners understood him.

As the gradually advancing, painstakingly prepared critical edition of the *Sermones* shows, the sermons present a theology that is thoroughly relevant even for present-day discussions. We also encounter this theology in Cusanus's numerous theological tracts. Rudolf Haubst, to whom we are indebted for opening up this theology, calls it "thinking belief and believing thought." Fundamental themes are: "God 'above' and 'in' the world as his creation"; "the human being's experience of self" as the starting point to "Jesus Christ as the fulfillment of the human being and the universe"; and last but not least, "the ecumenical meaning of the structure of the church of Jesus Christ." While all of this is impressively relevant, we admire no less Cusanus's theological erudition that brings together 1,500 years of Christian theology and at the same time leads further beyond.

Benefices

We find Nicholas back in Kues on February 1, 1425. This is his first return home for which we have proof. On the preceding day the Archbishop of Trier, Otto von Ziegenhain, had transferred the parish church at Altrich to him. With it came a handsome income. The church, under the authority of Wittlich, was not far from Kues. Nicholas entered into the service of the spiritual head of Trier, and in the summer of 1427 he stayed at the Trier **curia** as his **procurator**. From there he no doubt also pursued the cloister reforms that Otto promoted. At this time Nicholas called himself "Secretary to the Archbishop." Because of his service to the archdiocese Otto awarded him in 1430 an annuity of fifty gulden from the Office of the Seal in Koblenz.

Likewise, thanks to the archbishop Cusanus received, not least of all, numerous benefices that followed upon the transfer of Altrich. One was a **prebend** at St. Simeon in Trier in 1426; another was the parish church of St. Gangolf in Trier in 1427. As with Altrich, the authority to assign this church belonged to the archbishop. Cusanus was also named to the deanery of Our Lady in Oberwesel. This and St. Gangolf were temporary assignments, which meant that receiving the deanery with a prebend at St. Florin in Koblenz, where he took up residence, became all the more important. Then came a prebend in Karden in 1430, and a new one in St. Florin. During the same period he was already in possession of a prebend at St. Martin in Oberwesel, as well as of the position of **vicar** at the Mauritius Altar in the provost's quarters of St. Paulin in Trier.

The medieval system of benefices has had to suffer very sharp criticism. Devoutly offered donations and endowments served mainly to advance the material well being of the clerics, even though they did not fulfill the associated spiritual obligations. It was self-evident that when benefices at scattered locations were placed in the hands of one cleric, fulfillment of the various duties was illusory. Hence, the beneficed clergy installed vicars as substitutes, and, as a result, the endowed churches, chapels, and altars were first and foremost nothing more than objects of income. At the same time, the system provided a basic level of subsistence for many who, in the gradually increasing bureaucracy of the church, had to fill offices and perform assignments.

For these clergy the church was not acquainted with any other system than the political organization of the day in which people were compensated not with civil service wages, but with fiefs and benefices—that is, with material goods. This method naturally suggested itself for the administration of the church, though an alternative would have been for the church, in accordance with the demands of the poverty movement, to assume an absolutely spiritual form. It is true that in his correspondence Nicholas of Cusa posed as clearly as he could the question about renouncing earthly goods, but he balanced this with the counter-question of whether withdrawal from the world might mean withdrawal from responsibility for the world. He decided in favor of engagement with the world. However, then the task arises to decide how much of the income should go for personal use, how much for the material support of the institution, and, finally, how much for the response to the evangelical call for charity.

Conclusions about Cusanus's simple way of life free him from any suspicion of enriching himself personally. He asked himself very seriously whether it would not be better to distribute the abundant resources among the poor rather than spending them to increase the splendor and might of God's church. By applying all of his business and financial skills Nicholas, as Bishop of Brixen, managed to bring the bishopric, of which he was both spiritual and secular leader, out of debt and into a surplus that he utilized extensively. Yet God took everything from him and let the greedy Duke Sigismund triumph over him. In this hour Nicholas confessed that not until experiencing this loss had he become truly rich, because now he knew that it is more pleasing to God to give to the poor than to store up wealth in treasure chests. With the wish that everything God gave him should belong to those in need he established the endowment for a hospital in Kues for the poor.

Nevertheless, Nicholas continued his struggle for Brixen, not only in order to rescue his reform activity—which he thereby destroyed for the most part—but just as much to secure the material strength of his church. He believed that the prerequisite for the church to fulfill its spiritual mission was to be free of material need. Yet it was precisely the church's possessions that entangled him ever anew in unspiritual dealings.

The Path to Advancement

Nicholas was never squeamish about acquiring benefices and offices. His ambition, without which he never would have enjoyed such rapid advancement in the church hierarchy, pushed aside some who possibly had better claims. In a very short autobiography of 1449 Nicholas gives us a look at a kind of trauma that the lot of a bourgeois birth laid on him: he was fathered by a boatman from Kues, but the offspring nevertheless achieved great things, and eventually the popes recognized his accomplishments by elevating him to cardinal. "And this same cardinal has written this account for the praise of God in order that everyone should know that the Holy Roman Church cares neither about the place nor rank of one's birth, but rewards most generously only on the basis of one's virtues." Pride rings from these lines! See how far I, the son of a boatman from a remote place, have come!

We are indebted to Cusanus for one of the first maps of middle Europe. Eventually the map was credited to him, but without that discovery we would not suspect any connection between him and the map if it were not for the fact that the village of Kues is the only town shown between Trier and Koblenz, as though this were the most self-evident entry. Could the son of a Mosel River boatman have climbed to the rank of archbishop in Trier, Cologne, or anywhere else in the old empire where, in the cathedral chapters, the exclusivity of class would have excluded him? Here and there a middle-class person could achieve a high position of considerable influence, but the determining factor for the highest ranks of society was the aristocratic blood of one's father. Hence, Cusanus's thanks to the Roman Church for valuing merit, not origins! His feeling of inferior status was perhaps as strong as it was because he did not come from the lowest level of society, but from the midlevel patrician class that could match the nobility any time in achievement, culture, and intellectual horizons but was not allowed the same rights. Many wealthy citizens tried to rise above their class through "aristocratic" rights and through living like the nobility.

Pastor, Lawyer, Administrator

Nicholas tended tirelessly to the benefices entrusted to him. On the one hand, he looked after their material well being. The record of revenue from Cusanus's benefices was kept in the provost's register at Münstermaifeld. Whether out of a taste for financial management, out of enjoyment of money and profit, or out of a sense of duty Cusanus, after taking over the provost's office, worked his way through the register line by line, bringing the records up to date. As Prince-Bishop of Brixen he did the same thing with the thick registries of the lands and loans of the bishopric, and did it all in his own hand rather than leaving such a time-consuming task to his revenue collector.

More importantly, Cusanus dedicated himself passionately to the spiritual life of his institutions. St. Florin owes to him the first draft of a comprehensive set of statutes. Until then, as was the practice in other places, St. Florin had to make do with a conglomeration of individual rules and customary rights. As pastor of Bernkastel, he received permission from the pope in 1437 to introduce the Common Life among the clergy of his church. In doing so he confirmed specific regulations for clothing, living quarters, and duties in community living. One of the irritations he specifically named was the small size of benefices, and he tried to eliminate the problem by combining them.

Cusanus followed an improper practice of his day by holding

his church offices for a long time without being officially installed in them. The earliest he could have been ordained as a priest was 1436, yet the first sermon that has come down to us is one he had preached years before, in 1430. We will come across his pastoral zeal many times, but the universality of his intellect as well as his passion for far-reaching action could not be bound within the narrow confines of a pastoral office.

We also see Cusanus initially carrying out the practical duties of his academic career: in 1428 as mediator in a dispute about tithes at Nieder-Emmel on the Mosel, and in a dispute about burial rights in Boppard in 1432; in 1426 as legal counsel in a customs issue in Bacharach; in 1429 as assistant executor in a benefice trial in Limburg; and as legal advisor to the archbishop, whose Koblenz curia held its sessions in the cloister of St. Florin. Later in his *Invective* Heimburg scoffed at Nicholas, recalling that once he had soundly beaten Nicholas, the lawyer, in an inheritance trial in Mainz. Heimburg said this caused Nicholas to doubt his abilities in the practice of law, so he turned to theology, where he now intended to demonstrate the true faith through mathematical wizardry. It was hardly Nicholas's failure as a lawyer, but rather his universality—incomprehensible to his opponents—that of necessity broke the bounds of the specialists with the same result as when, at an earlier time, his broad educational interests had taken him beyond the narrow confines of an academic discipline.

Archival Research

In the spring of 1425 Nicholas matriculated at the University of Cologne as a Doctor of Canon Law. He probably held lectures in his field, but here, too, he left the traditional path. For one thing, he became a historian of law in a strict sense when, emulating similar efforts by Dietrich of Niem, he used not only codified law as a foundation, but also unearthed long forgotten sources of law in

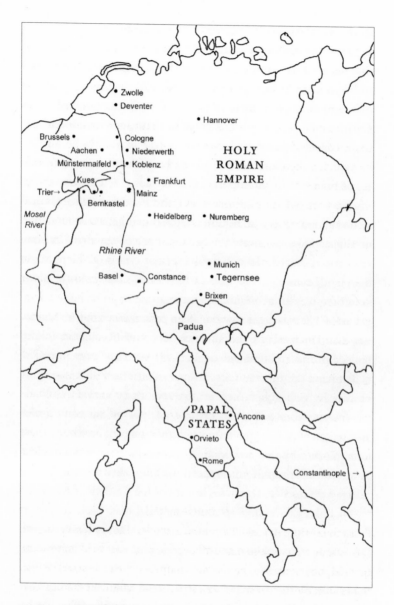

FIGURE 3. Map of Europe, 1400–1500, showing places connected with the life and career of Cusanus.

archives and libraries, and worked out their meaning for his day. Before the assembled Council of Basel he pointed out with pride that his legal support came not only from the familiar collections of law, but also from dust-covered original documents that he had pulled out of old cabinets. He referred with special emphasis to Germanic laws. Not only did he know that Charlemagne had had them collected and edited, but far more importantly, he himself had studied them one by one and had examined their application to the practice of contemporary law.

Drawing on legal history and critical sources, Nicholas furnished a masterpiece of argumentation proving that the Donation of Constantine—fabricated under the name of the first Christian emperor in order to legitimize the secular claims of the popes in the eighth century—had to be a forgery. He delivered the same kind of proof for pronouncements supposedly from Pope Clement and Pope Anacletus that had been passed down in the Pseudo-Isidorian **Decretals** of the ninth century. Nicholas's sources contained historical material no longer available to us. For example, he had at hand the report of a synod we otherwise would not know of that King Dagobert held in the seventh century in Cologne with twenty-four princes. Nicholas's analysis of old manuscripts aroused anxiety in opponents when they saw themselves backed into a corner by this new kind of approach, while it drew admiration from those who recognized his originality. Aeneas Sylvius referred expressly to this in his history of the Council of Basel.

Nicholas's collecting of source material goes back at least as far as to his time in Cologne. In the cathedral library he discovered the *Codex Carolinus*, the manuscript preserved today in Vienna containing papal letters to the Franconian rulers. In Cologne he also found official documents of the **Provincial** Council of Arles held in 417–418 that he later used in *The Catholic Concordance*. In 1428 he discovered in the cathedral library at Laon the famous *Libri Caro-*

lini with which Charlemagne had intervened quite self-confidently in doctrinal disputes of the church. Not until the sixteenth century did people again take notice of this work.

Nicholas of Cusa had a keen sense of what was historically important. He began with the source material and used it to clarify problems facing the church by revealing, in the end, how these were tied to their specific historical circumstances. His reputation as a scholar grew by leaps and bounds. In December 1428, while he was staying in Cologne, the city of Louvain offered him a chair in canon law at its newly established university. The city repeated its offer in 1435. In turning it down both times Nicholas demonstrated his intention, despite all his success, not to go down in history as a skilled academician.

The Influence of Heymeric, Albertus, and Llull

Should we not expect that in Cologne, as before in Padua, Cusanus directed his gaze far beyond the borders of his discipline? Indeed he did, for we see him eagerly engaged in theology and philosophy. The friend who inspired and encouraged him in this was Heymeric de Campo, six years older than Cusanus. Of the three dominant schools in Paris Heymeric had chosen to follow neither the Thomists nor the *via moderna* of the Ockhamists but the tradition of Albertus Magnus, who brought to the late Middle Ages an Aristotelianism shaped by Neoplatonism. This school held the view that being was much more dynamic than Thomism thought it to be. Heymeric, a member of the Cologne faculty of arts beginning in 1422, lectured as professor of theology from 1428 on, interrupted by three years of activity at the Council of Basel, until he was called to Louvain in 1435. There he was the dominating scholarly figure until his death in 1460.

Most likely it is from Heymeric that Cusanus became acquainted with the ideas of Pseudo-Dionysius (the Areopagite). This figure is the supposed pupil of the apostle Paul to whom the Christian-Platonic tradition of the Middle Ages traced itself without knowing that his thought had not been written down until approximately the year 500. Albertus Magnus wrote a commentary on Pseudo-Dionysius, Heymeric carried on the interest, and then the young scholar from Kues discovered in the Albertinian tradition one of the basic concepts that shaped his thinking, namely, the "coincidence of opposites," or *coincidentia oppositorum*. Cusanus's coincidence doctrine—we will come back to it later—was naturally anything but the philosophical trademark of Albertism. Albert spoke of coincidence within a realm of being whose causalities he collapsed into one. Cusanus expands the concept into the realm of being and non-being, and from there takes it even further to the last metaphysical possibility. In one of his glosses in Albert's commentary on Dionysius, Cusanus regrets that the great teacher did not draw God into his consideration of coincidence, but in this regard he could just as well have named Heymeric, who stimulated him to productive thinking.

Heymeric, in consonance with the Pseudo-Areopagite, taught the necessity to stride through the shadow of negation in order to reach the light of true understanding. Light symbolism was joined by the no less important symbolism of figures. With the figure of the sphere Heymeric portrayed the convergence in God of the causalities of action, form, and purpose. A sphere's center, diameter, and circumference served as symbols of the divine causes. In general, Heymeric loved to elucidate his teaching by means of geometric symbols. Building on Albert's precedent he elaborated the symbolism of the circle. He compared the relation between the oneness of what is uncreated and the multiplicity of what has been created to the circle being made up of all polygons.

A much stronger influence on Nicholas's number and figure

symbolism came from another source. In the thirteenth century the Catalan, Ramon Llull, had constructed in his remarkable *Great Art (Ars generalis)* a general theory of order by using symbolic geometrical figures and a system of general relations, applying exacting logic to cabalistic analysis of combinations. No medieval thinker is better represented in Cusanus's extensive library than Llull. Many copies of his works come from the hand of Cusanus. Numerous excerpts, glosses, and notes are evidence of the singular significance he attached to the great Catalan. Nicholas began writing out these excerpts and copies in 1428 when he was staying in Paris. Nicholas's Llullism carried on the work of the Parisian Llull circle that had formed around the Carthusian monastery of Vauvert. Heymeric, who was closely connected with Parisian academic life, played the role of go-between. One of the early notes about Llull's *Ars generalis,* in connection with an *Ars generalis* written under a pseudonym, appears in Cusanus's notes on Heymeric.

Nicholas's occupation with Llull first becomes evident at the end of the 1420s. This is only the beginning of a lifelong, stimulating influence, and *concordantia,* one of the fundamental concepts in Nicholas's thought—and action!—can well be credited to this influence. In Llull he found the concept defined this way: concordance is when goodness, greatness, and so on, are congruent in the one and the many. The only difference between this definition and the definition in *The Catholic Concordance* is the application of this principle to the nature of the church. Concordance is when the Catholic Church is congruent in the one and the many.

A part of Nicholas's character was his special liking for numbers and patterns in their creative, generative effect. Llull's influence lifted this interest to the height of speculative success. Eventually in his work *On Conjectures (De coniecturis)* Nicholas placed Llull's *Ars generalis* alongside his own *Ars coniecturalis.* In so doing the difference between his and Llull's appreciation for symbols becomes apparent: Nicholas's view is that they can never provide metaphysical proof with final certainty. What mattered for Llull was the strictest possible rational line of argumentation. Nicholas accepted nothing but the "word" as the only unqualified representation of all things. For this reason he indeed had a high opinion of the method Llull used in his *Ars generalis.*

The method of concordance—in combination with its antithesis, namely, argumentation on the basis of "difference," of noncongruence, also taken from Llull—furnished the basis for the *Ars coniecturalis,* the "art of conjecture." For only if everything corresponds to everything and yet is different from everything can everything serve as a symbol of something else. Creation becomes the reflection of God. The basic qualities that converge in him accrue secondarily, analogously, to all of creation. In the case of Llull, the "ternary," which takes on a geometric image in the triangle, became the starting point for a comprehensive interpretation of being. He dedicated his most intense effort to this when he grappled with the mystery of the divine Trinity. Connected with this was the theology of the circle: all divine attributes and correlatives are identical in their circular form.

Let us not overlook, however, that it was the intellectual background of Christian Platonism whose light shone through this entire tradition, and in its overall influence gave Nicholas's thinking its basic tone and determined his place in the history of the search for knowledge in the western world. The principle of "concordance and difference" appears in a Boethius commentary from the school at Chartres, and Nicholas was definitely acquainted with this commentary. The concepts of coincidence and concordance bring to the fore, as a fundamental issue of this Platonism, the question of unity, of comprehending the unity of God and creation and its stunning variety. This question will come to have nothing short of personal significance for Nicholas of Cusa. Let us not forget this when a flash of insight, that gift given to geniuses, opens up for him a view into the deeper connections of life.

However, this hour of fruitful inspiration that Cusanus himself regarded as God-given was still a decade away. The 1420s had blessed him with the unsuspected opportunity for a wealth of knowledge and understanding, but that period was still to be characterized by excerpts and notes. In eighteen sermons that have come down to us from the 1430s, we can see the effort with which he continued to press forward in his thinking. However, the Cusanus of these years was not yet the great philosopher. He was far more the man of canon law, of constitutional law, the author of *The Catholic Concordance,* and last but not least the personally engaged politician.

Early Fame as a Manuscript Collector

In these years, however, Nicholas was to make a name for himself in an entirely different area. During his search in archives and libraries he came across numerous manuscripts of classical Latin writers. Feverish excitement spread among the Italian humanists when they found out about his discoveries. During a stay at the Curia in 1427 he told the manuscript collector, Poggio, about Pliny's histories and Cicero's *Republic* that he said he had found in Germany. Since shortly before this Winand von Steeg, a secretary of the Cardinal Legate Giordano Orsini, believed he had discovered the *Republic* in a "dusty library" in Cologne, we can look in Cologne for the source of Nicholas's discoveries as well. Ulrich von Manderscheid was dean of the cathedral in Cologne. He certainly made the cathedral library available to Nicholas, who drew from its treasures. Two older brothers of Ulrich were members of the Cologne chapter as well, and upon closer examination we discover a number of other personalities whose favor was beneficial to Nicholas.

Poggio accepted the report with a certain amount of skepticism. In fact, two years later Nicholas had to admit that instead of the *Republic* he had found only Macrobius's already well-known commentary on *Scipio's Dream* (*Somnium Scipionis*). Nicholas compensated the humanists for this with twelve comedies of Plautus that no one had known about until then. Nicholas was skillful enough to be stingy with his treasures, and handed the manuscript over to Orsini, who guarded it carefully from the humanists, but then had copies made for the libraries of the princes of Florence, Milan, and Ferrara. Poggio intimated what reward was in store for Nicholas when he expressed his fear that he would lose all the treasures because the discoverer was not receiving any benefices from the pope. However, not long thereafter the confirmation of benefices flowed in great abundance, along with the necessary disbursements from the accumulated sources.

Beyond this, Nicholas used the opportunity in order to develop stronger personal support from the curial officials associated with the humanists. Soon they came in great numbers to the Council of Basel where Nicholas could take advantage of his connections. Present were Cardinal Nicholas Albergati and his secretary, Thomas Parentucelli, later Pope Nicholas V; Aeneas Sylvius Piccolomini, later Pius II, to whom he was bound in friendship and gratitude; Francesco Pizolpasso, bishop of Pavia and then archbishop of Milan, and his predecessor there, Archbishop Bartholomew de la Capra; Ambrose Traversari, **Prior General** of the Camaldolese; and many others. They flattered and courted him. Pizolpasso discussed philosophical and theological questions with his "dearest and most beloved" Nicholas.

Nicholas is the one who arranged for the manuscript of Donatus's commentary on Terence to be brought to Italy. Giovanni Aurispa, the scholar of Greek in the Florentine circle of humanists, had discovered the manuscript in Mainz in 1433. To enumerate here all the works Nicholas procured for the humanists would lead us too far astray. In the history of the study of the ancient world he secured a considerable name for himself. Nevertheless, it is doubtful whether he possessed the basic literary disposition that inspired his contemporary humanists. No doubt his thought and life were much too speculative, too metaphysical for him to find fulfillment in their literary world. Indeed, he did not exhaust his interests by searching for old manuscripts with literary, linguistic, and grammatical texts. His universal mind was suited to a far greater extent for collecting manuscripts with theological, philosophical, judicial, astronomical, and medical content. In one telling way he was on common ground with the humanists: in their love of books. He took great pleasure in the outward beauty of aesthetically pleasing manuscripts, and with the enthusiasm of a bibliophile he collected, along with more modest copies of works in common use, a number of magnificent editions that still today are among the precious objects in his library.

The Manderscheid Case

The Archbishop of Trier died at the beginning of 1430. The majority of the chapter elected Jacob von Sierck, a cathedral canon, to be his successor. Two votes went to Ulrich von Manderscheid, who had just turned thirty. Both candidates went to Rome, each wishing to receive the pope's confirmation. However, Martin V appointed Raban of Helmstadt, who had been Bishop of Speyer. Ulrich did not heed the ruling. Instead he used pressure and force in the chapter as well as in the archbishopric in order to assert himself as the new ruler. The pope excommunicated him and his supporters. A struggle erupted that lasted for years and led to war and devastation. Turned away by the Curia, Ulrich sought to win over the Council of Basel for his interests against the pope. He approached the council at the beginning of 1432, not long after it had opened.

Defending his position at the council was his personal advisor, secretary, and agent, Nicholas of Cusa.

In honoring Nicholas with this position of trust Ulrich was making a clever choice. His secretary's name was already widely known, not least of all among the German princes, in whose circle Ulrich, the not yet consecrated man from Trier, moved. Already in 1426 Nicholas had testified before Archbishop Dietrich of Cologne and Ludwig of the Palatinate in regard to an appeal by the Duke of Cleves. In 1432 Duke William of Bavaria, Protector of the Council, sent Nicholas as the matrimonial agent to the same Duke of Cleves, whose daughter Duke William, a Wittelsbacher, wished to have as his wife. In 1433 Nicholas was among the legal scholars who rendered an opinion for Duke William in his dispute with his brother, Duke Ernst.

The opposing side attacked Nicholas with biting misrepresentations and declared him to be the real cause of the entire dispute about Trier. In reality, Ulrich's claim rested alone on the power of a group of nobles, led by Count Ruprecht of Virneburg, who dominated the bishopric. This group wanted to secure for itself the deciding influence in the electoral state, a desire to be understood in the context of late medieval trends in the estates. In Nicholas the nobility found the theoretician who offered the legitimizing legal foundation for their endeavors, namely his doctrine of the laity's rights in the church.

Proceeding from the doctrine of consensus, and reaching beyond it to the general principle that everyone is by nature free, Nicholas maintained that a ruler cannot be forced upon anyone against his or her will. Consequently, he justified Ulrich's claim to the archbishop's seat by citing the wish of the laity. Yet he did not view the laity as a democratic electorate. Rather he considered the laity to be divided into a hierarchy of class groupings. It remains an open question whether in doing this he was conforming to the reality of Trier and to common perceptions about the structure of society in the late Middle Ages or whether he was convinced of a fundamental, divinely-ordered class structure of society.

Then in front of the forum in Basel that represented a universal public Nicholas, as Ulrich's advocate, elevated the seemingly local argument regarding Trier to the level of a paradigmatic case. He connected it with many of the pressing political, legal, and societal problems of the day. He linked his demand for consensus of the laity with the question of the extent to which Rome was justified in intervening in the filling of church offices, and the extent to which the issue of Trier was not ultimately a matter for the emperor. The pope was manipulating an electoral vote, and one of the empire's principalities was being occupied by means of an outside authority.

Ulrich's position lent itself very advantageously to publicity that characterized him as a martyr of the Curia's policy that was hated because of the *Gravamina*—oppressive measures—that it imposed on the German nation.

At the council Nicholas also touched not least of all on national pride. We do not know whether he was more serious about this than the doubtfulness of the claim he was defending would lead us to suspect, but he dearly loved his homeland, the German nation and the empire. When he had risen to the highest ecclesiastical ranks he repeatedly expressed his responsibility to his nation in particular. He did not let the heart that beat for it be buried in Rome. It was his wish that no matter where he died his heart should be brought back to Kues. There it was placed beneath the chapel floor.

The council fathers, who insisted on the rights of their nations, were probably moved less by the appeal to emotion than by the well-grounded political argument offered them in Basel. After lengthy urging by Cusanus proceedings were finally initiated in 1433. When they reached their final stage in May 1434, French representatives also joined in. They pointed specifically to the freedoms that would have to be secured for the national churches. For a few days Nicholas figured in the story of Gallicanism, the movement for authority of a national church. Yet even with the general sympathy he enjoyed in the council—despite his candidate's human and political failure, and despite hostility from Speyer—he did not achieve success. On May 15, 1434, the council declared Raban of Helmstadt, the pope's appointee, the lawful archbishop of Trier. Ulrich continued to fight, still advised by Nicholas, who for his own part submitted to the decision of the council. Yet by the end of 1435 Ulrich had gained only insignificant compensation for the claims he had presented. To be sure, Raban assumed a miserable inheritance because five years of strife had ruined the territory. Three years later he voluntarily withdrew.

A Rising Star in the Council of Basel

Nicholas gradually pushed his way up to the front rows at the council. The tasks assigned to him attest to his growing influence. Upon being incorporated into the council on February 29, 1432, he was assigned to the Commission on Matters of Faith. One year later we see him, among other things, as translator for the Protector of the Council, Duke William of Bavaria. We also find him in conversation about doctrine with the Bohemian representatives to the council who were in Basel to negotiate the return of the Hussites to the Catholic Church. Nicholas presented a compromise plan: henceforth the Bohemians would be allowed to receive communion in both kinds if they would give up their other demands. These demands were the freedom to preach, punishment of mortal sins, and evangelical poverty of the clergy. According to Nicholas, only the article about communion dealt with doctrine, while the other three were merely matters of discipline. However, the Hussites did not agree to the devaluation of these three articles and rejected his compromise. Later, of course, his proposal became the basis for the settlement reached in 1436.

It would seem as though Nicholas's treatise of 1433, *Communion under Both Kinds* (*De communione sub utraque specie*), hardly fits into this context. He calls upon the Bohemians to unite with the Roman Church. Yet this does not contradict the compromise he proposed because he assumes the Roman Church will recognize it. Naturally, he believes that communion, understood as a sacrament of unity, is always to be administered in unity. On the other hand, in the course of history the formal practice of communion has indeed changed. Thus, in the Bohemian treatise Cusanus leaves fully open the solution to the problem, as long as it does not contravene the uppermost precept of unity.

If any problem of the church was of supreme importance to Nicholas, it was, along with his demand for purity, the need for unity. At issue in winning back the Bohemians after John Hus broke away and was burned at the stake in 1415 was the unity of the church. The search for this unity went beyond the alternative, pope or council, to the only possible answer: pope *and* church, head *and* members. The necessity for unity with the Chair of Peter (*cathedra Petri*) that he stressed so heavily in the Bohemian treatise will reappear in *The Catholic Concordance,* making the *cathedra* often enough a prisoner in the chains of this necessity.

From the start, the Commission on Matters of Faith had to deal with the fundamental problem of the relationship to the pope. Before the council had actually begun, Pope Eugenius IV dissolved it in December 1431. Not until under pressure from Emperor Sigismund, whom he had crowned in Rome in May 1433, did he agree to recognize the council, an action he took on August 1, 1433. Then, however, he rejected as unacceptable the council's decree to exclude the Curia from the entire system of benefices. Cusanus belonged to the subcommittee whose task it was to deal with the papal **Bull of Submission**. The council declared the Bull to be inadequate, yet it hesitated to suspend the pope. Finally Eugenius yielded, and on December 15, 1433, he gave in without qualification to the demands of the council.

While the council recognized the pope, the question arose immediately as to what place the papal legates should occupy in the council. Nicholas of Cusa entered the discussion with his treatise, *On Presidential Authority in a General Council* (*De auctoritate praesidendi in concilio generali*). Endeavoring to reconcile both parties, he proposed recognizing the legates as presidents while denying them any authority to make binding decisions. In this instance, too, the final solution, accepted on the initiative of the emperor in April 1434, corresponded to Cusanus's proposal. According to this proposal, the legates were admitted into the council with presidential rights, but they received no legally binding powers, and had to swear to the principle of the primacy of the council's authority. Even though this solution meant that the legates would speak only for themselves in order not to cause any prejudicial reduction of papal privilege, it assured the ongoing practical work of the council with the participation of the papal legates. As in the case of the Bohemian question, Cusanus's solution had proven to be useful. His success, even if only temporary, was evidence of the political instinct he had in such matters.

In October 1434 Nicholas was still at work as mediator on behalf of the German nation in the conflict between Spain and England. At the same time the Commission on Matters of Faith had assigned him, among other things, the task of preparing the decree on **simony**. After this, as Ulrich was defying the council's decision with force of arms, Nicholas returned home temporarily in 1435. On May 20, 1435, Pizolpasso took over the task of being representative in a benefice issue that the council had assigned to Nicholas.

After Nicholas had rescued whatever he could for Ulrich by

means of negotiations he returned to Basel. While in March 1436 Cusanus did turn down the office of judge of faith in the Commission on Matters of Faith, this decision does not yet inform us about his now more reserved attitude toward the council. In the same month he and the bishop of Augsburg were sent as council envoys to Würzburg in order to mediate disputes between the bishop of Würzburg and the count of Wertheim. On May 25 the envoys reported to a plenary session of the council. On the same day the German nation and the Commission on Matters of Faith assigned Nicholas the task of investigating what was happening in regard to the administration of indulgence income that had been designated for the Greeks.

On June 1 he was given the assignment of examining a dispensation that Cardinal Albergati had granted the mendicants. On the same day the council sent Cusanus and Johannes Schele, bishop of Lübeck, to Regensburg, where they negotiated a peace treaty between Margrave Frederick of Brandenburg and Duke Ludwig of Bavaria. Following this Nicholas was sent back to Würzburg on September 7. On September 22 the commission appointed him to deal with a petition from the bishop of Toul regarding reform statutes for the clergy in his diocese. In the same month he was appointed the council's reviewer of cases, and on October 5, 1436, the commission elected him curator of decrees.

Nicholas participated with special enthusiasm in the plans of the council for calendar reform and made very useful comments about it in his document, *Reform of the Calendar* (*De reparatione kalendarii*). His *Conjecture on the Last Days* (*Coniectura de ultimis diebus*), which appeared ten years later, reminds us how closely Nicholas was able to connect mathematical and astronomical seriousness with prognosticating number play that was a child of its time. In the work Nicholas calculated that the resurrection would occur between 1700 and 1734.

Looking at all the foregoing activities, the year 1436 exhibits Nicholas's most active engagement in the council. The negative decision by a slim majority against Ulrich von Manderscheid had not deterred him. Cusanus did not regard involvement in the council to be opportunism because the council put into practice his own convictions about the necessity for genuine representation of society.

Cusanus presented *The Catholic Concordance,* his first great work, to the council either at the end of 1433 or the beginning of 1434, and overnight it made him famous among those who had not yet taken notice of him. Regardless how closely his argumentation on behalf of Ulrich von Manderscheid before the council corresponded to his train of thought in *The Concordance,* this work towers far above mere service for a pragmatic goal. The fact that sentences in *The Concordance* appear verbatim in the proceedings of the Trier dispute indicates at most how rigorously Nicholas turned theory into practice.

The Catholic Concordance

The Catholic Concordance had occupied Nicholas during 1433. He preceded it in the spring of that year with a work *On the Greater Authority of the Sacred Councils over the Authority of the Pope* (*De maioritate auctoritatis sacrorum conciliorum supra auctoritatem papae*). As in the case of his treatise on the Bohemians, he proceeds above all historically. He shows how in the course of history the council evolved in its representation of the whole church. The whole church consists of nothing less than all five patriarchates: Rome, Constantinople, Alexandria, Antioch, and Jerusalem. Hence, any council that is limited to the West, even though it might designate itself as "general," must keep in mind its particularity as a council of the Roman patriarchate. Of course, this approach does not produce an answer to the issue contained in the title of the work, so in the more extensive study represented by *The Catholic Concor-*

dance Nicholas goes beyond the historical dimension to a synthesis that ties together theology and law, history and practice. This synthesis is meant to clarify the problem without being a for-or-against decision.

The Catholic Concordance underwent numerous revisions and expansions, and Nicholas's repeated starts, reorganizations, and additions are evidence of the great difficulty of the task. In the final analysis, the basic issue seemed to him to be absolutely irresolvable in isolation. What he had undertaken as a special examination of the superiority of the council grew, as he wrote, into a general examination of the societal issues of his day. At first he turned his attention only to the structure of the church. In doing so he placed the pope-council issue on the foundation of the doctrine of consensus.

It was probably the arrival of the emperor at the council in October 1433 that motivated him to investigate reform of the empire. Not until then did he harmoniously connect body and soul, state and church in the organism of Christian society in order to arrive at a comprehensive diagnosis and recommendation for treatment. In a hymn-like tribute he celebrates Sigismund as the rescuer awaited by all, as the one who will lead them into a prosperous future. In viewing all societal questions from the highest vantage point, and in conceptualizing them in the context of the structure of the entire universe Nicholas's study towers far above all other comparable works of the conciliar epoch. *The Catholic Concordance* has been called the last great work in the history of political theory prior to Machiavelli's *Prince*. No comparison could better exemplify the radical change in that era.

For Cusanus the universe is constructed hierarchically. By nature every being occupies a place assigned to it within the great order of the universe. All beings are held in a system of divine relationships that are revealed in the correspondence between the heav-

43

enly and earthly that pervades everything. The steps of the heavenly hierarchy are repeated in the hierarchy of the church, and in it the spiritual and secular order unfolds in matching ranks of rulers that can be traced out in a pattern of ever finer branches. One does not need Nicholas's specific reference to Pseudo-Dionysius in order to recognize that he embeds *The Catholic Concordance* in the neoplatonic system of thought. At first glance one could dismiss the complicated triadic thought that leads far beyond Pseudo-Dionysius as a frivolous game. Yet we can see in it the serious attempt at a new symbolic ecclesiology that, freeing itself from scholasticism, wants to develop a deeper and broader understanding of the church.

Thus, in Cusanus's view we discover a cosmos, a world organized according to numbers and degree, level and rank. In Machiavelli's view, on the other hand, we find the absolute right of the individual in the state, and reasons of state as the basis of an existence that is left to fend for itself and is engaged at most in a game of forces that move about next to each other.

Yet history does not happen overnight. What is growing now will unfold one day in full blossom. Powerful blows battered the age of hierarchical thinking. The democratic, pluralistic principle that no longer constructed the social order like one hierarchical pyramid demanded to be heard, even if the future was not to belong to it until much later. The democratic principle proceeded from equality, equal rights, and the equal worth of all, this worth being endowed as a natural right—a view that the Stoic system of thought transmitted down through the years in the Christian tradition. In the history of political theory the democratic principle found its first practical formulation in the principle of the consent that subjects give to their ruler and his government.

If one wants to seek out Cusanus's basic question, then one finds it here in all clarity: how, in fact, is one to comprehend the right of the many, of the "infinity of little things," as Leibnitz called them, when they belong to an integrated whole? How do the microcosms relate to the macrocosm? The tension that this basic question produced kept Cusanus, the philosopher, in suspense to the same degree that it kept Cusanus, the theologian and political theoretician, in suspense. So, too, it affected Cusanus, the person struggling with events of the time, and finally Cusanus, the person needing to attend to the aggravating little worries of everyday life while seemingly greater tasks had to wait. The attempt to resolve this tension, to master it with the comprehensive understanding of correspondence, of "concordance," found its most eloquent expression in the title he gave to his first great work. *Condordantia catholica* is the name of his life's program.

The Principle of Concordance

In the principle of concordance Nicholas brought together two intellectual streams: on the one hand, canon law developed over time primarily by the councils, and, on the other hand, medieval Neoplatonism in its manifold expressions. In a simplifying, but not exhausting way, one can say that the neoplatonic stream transmitted the element of unity, while the canonistic tradition set forth the problem of multiplicity. We have already noted the great variety of contacts Cusanus had with both of these intellectual worlds.

Cusanus's division of *The Catholic Concordance* into three books almost has the effect of a blueprint, for it presents three books that in trinitarian unfolding treat the spirit (sacrament), soul (priests), and body (people) of the church. Three—the number full of significance in theology as well as in mathematics—is here, too, in the doctrine on Christian society! At the same time the ternary in the microcosm of the human being points to the following analogy: the naturally unfolding abundance of things within the individual is like the corresponding organic fashioning of the societal macrocosm. Cusanus accepted the tradition of thinking in terms

45

of an organism. This offered him the possibility of bringing together in a fruitful synthesis multiplicity and unity in the dynamic process of unfolding and reuniting. Unity is not to subjugate multiplicity in heartless servitude, but is meant to bring it to completion. Multiplicity is not to shatter unity pluralistically, but is meant to reflect in infinite refractions the ground of being contained in it.

The Catholic Concordance represents not only the most broad-reaching résumé of medieval theories of society, but at the same time, because of its immersion in philosophical-theological speculation, the most original achievement. Perhaps coming closest to it in his reasoning about constitutional law is the conciliar theoretician of the previous generation, Pierre d'Ailly. He, in similar fashion, worked on resolving the tension between hierarchy and consensus. A hundred years earlier in his book *On Conducting a General Council,* William Durant the Younger had already characterized the pope and bishops together as the proper lawgiving authority of the church, governing it in concord under the inspiration of the Holy Spirit. Pierre d'Ailly further delineates the practical possibilities. In place of the bishops, the cardinals—as the standing representatives of the ecclesiastical provinces—are, together with the pope, to govern the church in harmonious agreement of head and members. Nicholas adopted this concept as well as the distinction d'Ailly had worked out between the pope's function as head of the universal church and shepherd of the Roman Church (*ecclesia Romana*). Yet the larger context into which Nicholas places all of this, connecting the canonistic tradition with the ideas handed down by the neoplatonic tradition, is already much more strongly suggested by a kindred spirit, Jean Gerson. Due to its theological-philosophical reflections, the council's discussion in the fifteenth century avoids, to a great extent, being purely legalistic argumentation. We see in Heymeric de Campo, John of Torquemada and John of Segovia indications of this orientation, one in which

Cusanus's work takes its place, though towering above the others.

For Cusanus the principle of concordance possessed dynamic vitality and had a wondrously life-generating effect: "From the one king of peace who is supported by unlimited harmony flows that sweet, blended spiritual harmony step by step, little by little, into all members who are subject to him and united with him, just as the one God is everything in everything." How far this perception of the living organism of society is removed from concepts of democracy that restrict themselves to a highly formal constitutional mechanism needs no explanation. His view not only affirms human freedom that is rooted in natural rights, but allows it to blossom in a positive way. Nicholas finds the most solid basis for consensus in the spiritual marriage of Christ with his church.

Nicholas not only speculated from lofty heights, but he also kept concrete needs before his eyes. Having concluded that an elected monarchy arising inevitably from the combination of the concepts of hierarchy and consensus was the best form of government, he proceeded to make detailed recommendations for securing peace and order in the realm. He supported the reform measures being called for from many sides, the introduction of an imperial army, an imperial tax, the formation of imperial courts of justice to guarantee domestic peace, and the creation of a uniform body of German law.

However, these proposals, unlike others that Cusanus had crafted in such a way that they resulted in very successful compromises, went beyond what had any chance of being approved. *The Catholic Concordance* reveals Cusanus's desire that took shape under the motto "reform," but that demanded too much and stood in opposition to the circumstances of the day. In his zeal for reform Nicholas proved only too often to be fruitlessly rigid. Although he obviously overestimated what could be accomplished, his persistence to do what he thought was right speaks well of him. Be that as it may, the divergence between wish and reality awakened in him deep doubts about the actual achievability of what he recognized as right. These doubts manifested themselves from time to time in a tolerance that was too generous, and then they would stiffen into an uncompromising hardness that some contemporaries thought was characteristic of him. "Concordance," the harmony of feelings and impulses—yet how often outbreaks of anger and tears!—the harmony of thoughts and decisions—yet how many contradictions!—became for the one who was plagued by tensions within himself not only a lesson to teach, but a lesson to live.

Church and Council

Along with his concern about the empire Nicholas's main purpose in writing *The Catholic Concordance* is the one that had prompted him from the start: to clarify the relationship between pope and council. He sets out on a search for the church. To whom was the promise given that the church's founder would be with it until the end of time? Who is the church? Not the pope, because he, as pope, is not infallible. The Roman Church? No doubt, if it is understood as the entire church. At first this appears to be a meaningless tautology: the church is the church. Yet the root of the solution to the problem lies precisely in this definition, and one gets at the root by means of the counter-question about the infallibility of the council.

Nicholas differentiates between the universal council of all Christianity and the patriarchal councils under the patriarchs. One of the patriarchs, along with those of the East, is the bishop of Rome. The universal council is above the pope, the patriarchal council is under him. The universal council is not infallible in every case, although it is less fallible than the pope. However, the patriarchal council under the pope is infallible because the Roman See (*sedes Romana*) cannot err.

The pope has the prerogative to convene a council. If he holds back or refuses, then this duty falls to the emperor. However, the council cannot pass any resolutions in matters of faith without listening to the pope, because certainty is ensured only through unanimity. This does not hold true if the pope is heretical. For this reason the council cannot suspend him, as happened in Basel, for either he is the pope with all his authority, or he is no longer pope as soon as he is a heretic. The universal council can dismiss the pope if he violates the duties of his office. The patriarchal council is under him and therefore can dismiss him only in case of heresy. Actually one cannot speak of a "dismissal." Rather, in committing heresy the pope dismisses himself, and the council merely announces this fact.

Still not clarified is the issue about the authority of the authority. The Council of Basel granted it to itself. It declared Eugenius IV heretical because he did not recognize the council's decrees and it elected a new pope, Felix V. Nicholas wanted a declaration like this to be valid only in the case of unanimity. Hence, the existence of a council minority withdrew legitimacy from the action of the majority. Just as a majority could not wield valid authority, neither could the pope by himself. The council was less fallible than the pope because it represented the church better than the bishop of Rome. According to Nicholas all the bishops together represent the totality of all churches. Yet they, too, are not infallible if they do not represent this totality as the Roman Church. Pope *and* council is Nicholas's answer to the question posed to him regarding pope and council as alternatives. No church without the connection to Rome!

This church is built from the bottom up, beginning with the local parish. Only vaguely, "muddled," does the pope represent the whole church, more distinctly does the Roman patriarchy, and most distinctly does the diocese. The church is in the bishop, whom the priests have chosen, and these, in turn, have been chosen by the believers. Thus, Nicholas, quoting the church father, Cyprian, desires to ground the church on a deeply based religious understanding of consensus.

Nicholas did not want this doctrine, which possibly could pass along to the laity considerable influence in the governance of the church, to be interpreted mechanically. The bishop certainly represents more than the sum of the consensus of his faithful. Nicholas emphasized the fundamental difference between laity and priests by adopting the conventional image of body and soul in the organism of the church. Priests can be removed only by their superiors. Here, in contrast to the voting process, the hierarchical principal is in effect.

In Basel Nicholas experienced how the majority unjustifiably granted itself an infallibility that tyrannized the opposing right of the minority. The majority acted illegitimately. Viewed from this perspective, Nicholas's development over the next few years as pope and council separated can be interpreted as being rather consistent. He learned to value authority, that is, the importance of the view from the top down. The accusation that Nicholas betrayed what he stood for is unfounded when one examines his views in *The Concordance* in their entirety. Nevertheless, some things Nicholas had expressed earlier about the authority of the universal council no doubt left a slightly bitter taste in his mouth. When in a sermon of 1440 he quoted once more from the *Ecclesiastical Concordance* (*Concordantia ecclesiastica*), he referred only to the hierarchical elements in it. He also did not include the work in the collection of his scholarly writings that he gathered into splendid codices at the end of his life.

Retreat from Basel

The new break between pope and council was initiated on June 9, 1435, when the council abolished all annates, pallium fees, and other assessments by the pope. Since the pope, threatened by unrest in Rome, had left the city under humiliating circumstances and was enjoying the hospitality of Florence, this action of the council completely outmaneuvered him. In June 1436 he appealed to the European public with bitter accusations against Basel. The conflict turned into a great test of power when the Greeks, seeking help from the West against the deadly threat from the superior Turkish might, traveled to Basel in order to prepare for unity negotiations. Who now represented the church, the pope or the council? Certainly it would be the one who would succeed in the work for unity.

The choice between the two became a concrete issue when it came to choosing a place for the negotiations. The council majority favored Basel, Avignon, or a place in Savoy. The minority, encouraged by the papal legates, wanted Florence, Udine, or any other Italian city acceptable to the pope. The ensuing resolution of December 9, 1436, led to a split in the council on May 7, 1437. On September 18, 1437, Eugenius IV transferred the council from Basel to Ferrara, where Cardinal Albergati, as papal legate, opened the first session on January 8, 1438.

Because of the Manderscheid affair Nicholas found himself in stronger opposition to the pope than he had ever desired or had regarded as justifiable. After all, following the first vote that gave Jacob von Sierck the majority, Ulrich von Manderscheid had sought recourse in the pope's authority. Evidence shows that Nicholas had renewed his contact with the Curia in 1435, or perhaps even earlier. At the beginning of 1435 his influence in Trier brought him the diocese of Münstermaifeld through the vote of the collegiate chapter there. On May 11, 1435, he applied to Eugenius IV for transfer of the diocese to him, though not until November 21, 1435, did he receive the corresponding approval when the council ratified his selection. As a supporter of Ulrich, Nicholas was at the time still excommunicated as far as the Curia was concerned, and he needed the intervention of Ambrose Traversari with the curial official, Bishop Christopher of Cervia, and perhaps also the help of other friends in order to dispel doubts about his person. The doubts dissipated after his excommunication was lifted, an action connected with the pope's acceptance of the compromise between Ulrich and Raban on March 7, 1436. Later, on October 25, 1436, Nicholas had Eugenius IV renew the assignment of all his benefices.

We see how cleverly Nicholas acted when he had to fight for ownership of the parish church of Bernkastel that had been assigned to him at least since 1436. Among those who disputed his right to the church was Hugo Dorre, Raban's chief attorney and Cusanus's embittered opponent in the Manderscheid affair. In contrast, a powerful friend stood up for him, the papal legate to the council, John Cervantes. He directed words of admonishment to Raban, who owed his archbishopric entirely to the pope, whereas both the pope and the council had transferred the church at Bernkastel as well as the diocese of Münstermaifeld to Nicholas. We might regard this game—using both sides, pope and council—as opportunistic, or we might see it as Nicholas's effort to have a sincere relationship with the Roman Church, whose importance for the entire church he had never denied. Either way, in Basel he would be able to maintain his position only temporarily.

On November 19, 1436, Nicholas, in the name of the German nation, tried to postpone the decision about where to meet the Greeks. In the vote on December 5 he went over to the side of the minority and became one of its leading advocates. He and the Bishops of Digne and Porto constituted the three-member delegation that left Basel in May 1437 for Bologna, where the pope was staying. They carried with them a copy of the decree, issued by the minority on May 7, 1437, about the chosen site, as well as letters from the council legate, Cesarini, to the emperor and patriarch of

Constantinople. In Bologna the pope was very pleased to affirm their mission, and on his behalf they were escorted by his nephew, Condulmer, archbishop of Tarentaise, and by Christopher Garatoni, bishop of Koron. After the Greek envoy had recognized the council minority under its papal-appointed president as the legitimate representative of the western church, the delegation set sail in August from Venice for Constantinople.

Interest in the Greek World

Nothing could have made Cusanus's prominent position in the church more apparent than his assignment to go to Constantinople. He could rightfully take pride in it. The defeat in the Manderscheid trial had left his reputation unscathed. However, it was not only his respected standing to which he owed his place in the legation to Constantinople, but above all, his special fascination with the Greek language. It had aroused lively interest precisely in 1437. Pizolpasso consulted Cusanus when translating the word *Areopag*, after having checked with Aurispa and then even with a Greek. "At last," Pizolpasso wrote, there is someone who "is well acquainted with the Greek language, and in other respects is very learned, a universal talent," and a "discoverer of innumerable manuscripts, owner, above all, of Greek works, among them some with Latin definitions of words and grammatical explanations." Naturally, works of this sort had to be especially valuable in the conversations with the Greeks.

Early Christian synods held in the East aroused Nicholas's special interest and became part of his sources for *The Catholic Concordance*. He brought back from Constantinople a Greek manuscript that contained the sixth to eighth councils. These were the Third and Fourth Councils of Constantinople of 680–681 and 869–870 and the Second Council of Nicea of 787. Cesarini, who on October 17, 1438, asked Ambrose Traversari for the return of the manuscript, characterized it as a valuable document for discussion with the Greeks about the *filioque* clause ["who proceeds from the Father *and the Son*"] in the Nicene Creed. The most fruitful result of Nicholas's familiarity with issues of dogma was an irenic spirit and sympathetic understanding that enabled him to see with ecumenical breadth beyond the narrow confines of western Christianity. Herein he took on the spirit of his humanistic friends who, possessing as little as he of the zealot's conversion impulse, were not interested in leading blinded heretics back into the arms of the mother church. Rather, in nonjudgmental appreciation of the faith and religious practices valued and preserved by the Eastern Church, they wanted to unite with brothers in a brotherly way. In *The Concordance* Cusanus gave the patriarchy of the East a place alongside Rome in the church structure. Bringing these together would represent more clearly what the church is. The trip must have seemed to Nicholas like carrying out a divine mandate.

Journey to Constantinople

Condulmer and Cusanus sailed first to Crete. There they picked up 300 crossbowmen who were to take over the protection of Constantinople when the emperor traveled to the West. A few days after they arrived in Constantinople a legation from the majority in the Council of Basel also reached the imperial city. The papal galleys would have attacked the legation had the emperor not intervened. By now Cusanus had a rather large personal retinue. It included a Johannes Bisscoping from Nordwalde near Münster, a Johannes Birck or Burck from Kues, a Gotfridus Habotey from Bastogne, brother of Cusanus's later secretary, Johann of Bastogne, a William Tant, and a Nicholas Wendelin, alias Zwarcz.

The effort to dispel the last reservations of the Greeks was a success. The Greeks did not follow the council majority, but rather the church that was represented by the pope and the College of Cardinals. Later, looking back on these talks, Nicholas offered them as proof that he had remained consistent in his position toward the pope. He said that he had told the Greeks the same thing that earlier he had told the Bohemians, namely, that they must be one with the Roman Church.

On November 27, 1437, the emperor and patriarch, along with the legates sent by the pope and the minority, set sail for the West. After a stormy voyage the fleet landed at Venice on February 8, 1438. The council of union opened in Ferrara on April 9. Nicholas, who along with the Bishop of Digne had hurried ahead to report to the pope, was present at Ferrara as one of those honored for their service and success. The pope worked on transferring the provostship of Magdeburg to Nicholas. Although the pope had assigned it to him on July 27, 1437, Nicholas had been unable to take possession of it. During the next year people addressed Nicholas as Provost of Magdeburg, but then he discontinued using this title.

The Gift from the Father of Light

An illustrious party from the East accompanied their emperor and patriarch. The most prominent figure was Bessarion, Archbishop of Nicea, one of the most erudite Greeks, who was to play an important role as mediator at the council. In 1439 he became a cardinal of the Roman Church. Under the Platonist, Gemistos Plethon, he had entered into the tradition of platonic philosophy. An untiring and experienced manuscript collector, he won the thanks of the West for rescuing numerous Greek codices. He learned Latin and became a translator of Greek works. Nicholas of Cusa became a lifelong friend of this kindred spirit. For example, Nicholas had a copy of Bessarion's translation of Aristotle's *Metaphysics*. This he gave to Bessarion in order that the Greek could correct it by comparing it line by line with his original translation. When Bessarion negotiated in Venice for a settlement with Duke Sigismund he proved to be kind and caring to Nicholas and was also helpful in obtaining income for him.

Along with Bessarion, the other leading prelates of the East participated in the journey. They were Mark Eugenicus, the archbishop of Ephesus; the bishops of Nicomedia and Trebizond; representatives of the patriarchates of Alexandria, Antioch, and Jerusalem; and the Grand Ecclesiarch Sylvester Syropoulus, who was to become the council's chronicler. In this company of travelers we find the German, the man with a universal background, yet knowledge-hungry, stimulating, yet eager to be stimulated! This is a man who intensifies existence through his awareness of the knowledge he possesses, a knowledge that maintains its credibility, is recognized, praised—and Nicholas, so confident in his knowledge thus praised, can safely become totally unassuming, and in admitting his not-knowing ascend to the most elevated level of thought, that of "learned not-knowing," of *docta ignorantia*. Added to this is his experience of the turbulent sea, of distance, of magnitude itself, and within this is the adventure in the tiny little dot of a ship threatened by danger! Thus, prepared by the atmosphere, circumstances, and timing to catch the divine spark, Nicholas receives "as a gift from above, from the father of light" the inspiration as to how human knowledge is to reach out and ascend toward the infinite.

Nicholas will confess that he struggled for years over how the mind can grasp the incomprehensible, but he never achieved success until this inspiration came to him. He will recall his teachers, his readings, his excerpts, and his notes, but having been seized by the power of revelation he will identify what he now has to say as something far more than a product of tradition. Nicholas was in Kues when he finished the last page of the manuscript *On Learned Ignorance (De docta ignorantia)*. It was February 12, 1440. He believed he was marking a date of significance, and it was also not

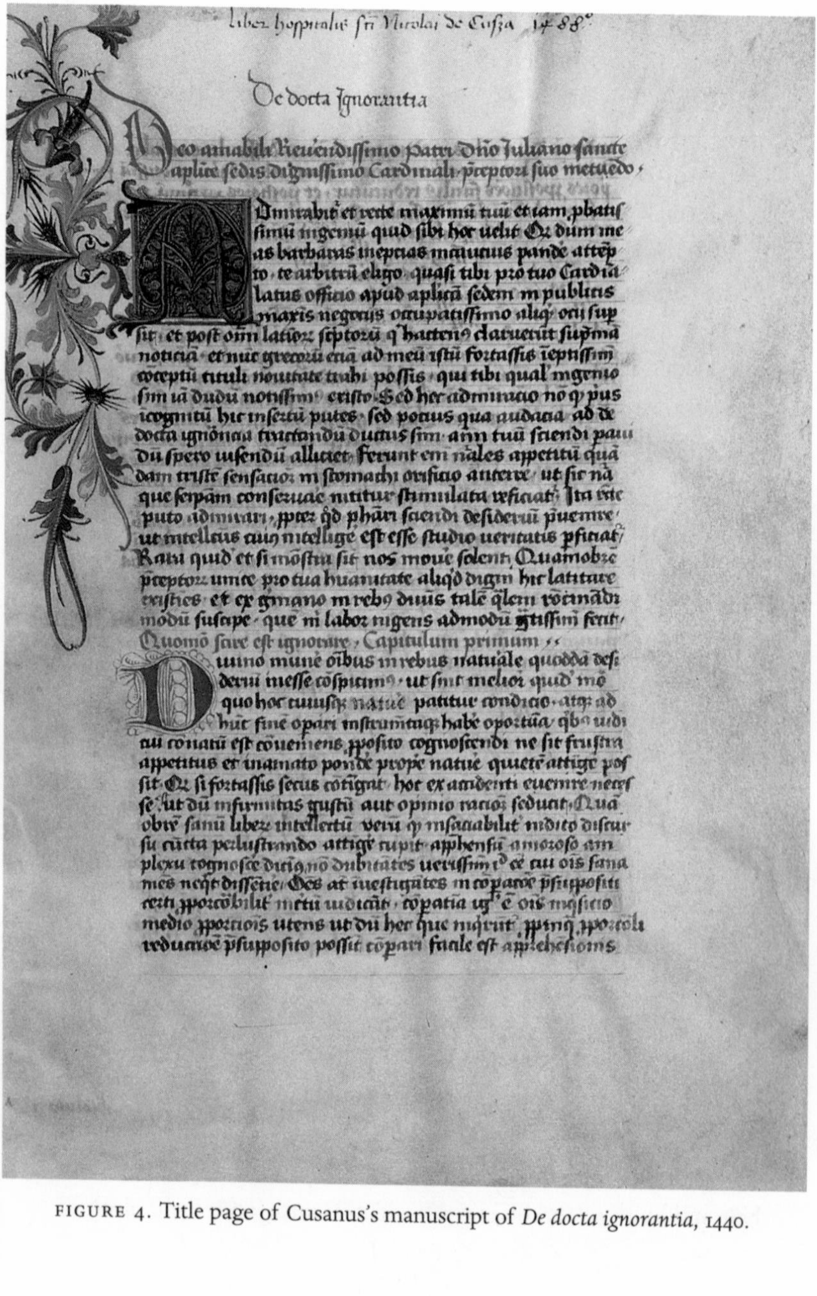

De docta Ignorantia

[Illuminated manuscript page of dense abbreviated Gothic Latin text, with decorative initials and marginal foliate ornamentation. The body text is the opening of Nicholas of Cusa's *De docta ignorantia*, beginning with a dedicatory address and the first chapter.]

Capitulum primum

Quomodo scire est ignorare.

FIGURE 4. Title page of Cusanus's manuscript of *De docta ignorantia*, 1440.

without pride that he added the word "Kues." Constantinople and Kues—what an enticing relationship to demonstrate the "coincidence of opposites," the great world contrasted with the point on the map where Cusanus's spirit had had its start.

Learned Ignorance

The speculation in Learned Ignorance begins with the question about oneness, or, more precisely, about the one, fundamental ground in which all multiplicity has its origin and which makes the interrelationship of multiplicity comprehensible. The neoplatonic tradition traced God and world, infinity and finite creation, back to an ultimate ground, but in doing so it often ended in pantheism and left to the Christian tradition the task of protecting God. In fact, after Nicholas published his work, Johannes Wenck, his opponent, challenged him on this point, but Nicholas, in his *Apology for Learned Ignorance (Apologia doctae ignorantiae)*, rejected Wenck's criticism.

Christian Neoplatonism affirmed God's transcendence through its "negative theology" that grants validity only to statements about God that reject characteristics with which we are acquainted. He is the complete other. Nicholas, still committed to this principle even as he went beyond the conventional concept of opposites, guarded himself against the pantheistic consequences. Wenck feared that Nicholas had not escaped them, but Wenck not only may have had an uneasy conscience, but he was also fundamentally a lesser intellect than Nicholas. Later Giordano Bruno also missed the mark, when, searching for a knowledgeable precursor in supposedly darker times, he misinterpreted Nicholas and consequently expressed unwarranted admiration for his pantheism.

But back to Nicholas himself! Knowledge begins with the recognition of the universal that underlies the multiplicity of discernable things. Therefore, our intellect must strive for the purest possible concept of oneness. The essence of oneness includes its simplicity. The simplest thing is the most certain. Thus, in order to attain knowledge that is certain one must proceed from oneness to differentiation, from simplicity to complexity, from the eternal to the transitory, and not vice versa.

Here at the beginning of Nicholas's argument knowledge is not the knowledge gained from experience. This is an important point for us to remember in order to keep in proper perspective what he emphasizes elsewhere, namely, to proceed from concrete experience. At the same time Nicholas does not want to deduce from abstract ideas, for oneness is not an idea, but God. Yet if this is the case, is knowledge even possible? We proceed logically from the known to the unknown, but progression in this manner all the way to God is impossible since between him and everything else is a gaping hiatus that thwarts any accessibility. Thus, God, the most certain thing, remains unknown to us. At this point Nicholas discovers the method of investigation that surpasses the usual way of comprehending. He calls it "comprehending incomprehensibly" (*incomprehensibiliter inquirere*).

This method consists of using symbols—geometric symbols—that are not encumbered with the uncertainty of the world of experience. They are by definition and due to their properties absolute and reliably discernable. A circle is with absolute certainty a curved line whose collective points are all exactly the same distance from one particular point. Here a world opens up for us that, through our certainty about it, allows us to reach towards God. At the same time, the similarity of the symbolic figures as well as of the mathematical relationships nevertheless ensure the diversity of content that they determine. For this reason mathematical symbols can be brought into play for knowledge of God, and while God's essence cannot be exhausted by them, they nevertheless are able to tell us something about him.

It follows then that dimensions and numbers furnish a reliable instrument superior to all others for increasing our understanding. Geometry offers itself to us as a strictly ordered and consistent "unfolding" world. Out of the straight line arises by way of the triangle the circle, and out of the circle, through its rotation in the third dimension, the most perfect of all bodies, the sphere. This movement, this "unfolding," is played out in the realm of finite dimensions with such absolute certainty that, of necessity, it demands the equivalent effect when the straight line is no longer a given length, but, exceeding all dimensions, is infinite. Then it is simultaneously the infinite triangle, the infinite circle, the infinite sphere, because the circle with the largest circumference is the least curved, and the least curved line is straight. Of course, our conceptual thinking cannot comprehend this convergence of infinite figures, yet reason compels us to acknowledge it.

With this we "touch" God's infinity, which, as absolute maximum, of necessity goes beyond all realms of being. Hence, everything must converge in this infiniteness. Indeed, infinity is all the greater once it is understood in contradictory fashion as finite, when everything that converges is all the more incompatible and all the more opposite. God's infinity is therefore the "coincidence of opposites" (*coincidentia oppositorum*). His infinity is more than the greatest; it is maximum and minimum at the same time. This is the highest possible form of knowing that we can attain, namely the analogous recognition of knowing that we do not know, and this lifts us beyond the boundary of the conceivable.

Apology for Learned Ignorance

The points we are noting here could not be accepted without objection if one wanted to preserve the absolute validity of the principle of contradiction in its customary sense. To be sure, Cusanus's efforts aimed precisely at overcoming contradiction or conflict, and, in fact, he was so intent on this aim that we thought we had recognized in it what had motivated him in the first place. However, the way in which *Learned Ignorance* attempted to solve the puzzle was dangerous, since it threatened to weaken the boundary between creator and creature if everything converged in God. Cusanus recognized this danger immediately and with penetrating argumentation called into question the correctness of a pure metaphysics of being that he had just come across in the works of Meister Eckhart. We know that Cusanus occupied himself with Meister Eckhart over the next few years because a copy of Eckhart's *Three-part Work* (*Opus tripartitum*) from 1444 contains numerous marginal notes from Cusanus. In his *Apology for Learned Ignorance* (*Apologia doctae ignorantiae*, 1449) Cusanus defends Eckhart against the accusation of pantheism.

Perhaps it is precisely in analyzing Eckhart that Nicholas came to the development and final formulation of his clarifying answer to the question raised in *Learned Ignorance*. He warded off the danger of pantheism by removing the existence of God from the abstraction of the intellect. Eckhart transferred monistically the finite way of thinking to the subject at hand. The impossibility of "clearing up" the dualism led him to the impossibility of dualism at all. In contrast, Nicholas, by recognizing the limits of understanding, achieved a critical distance and objectivity. In this way his obsessive hunt for paradoxical formulas, as expressed with the "coincidence of opposites," led by way of his fundamental recognition of the insufficiency of any intellectual solution to his solid experience of a metaphysical transcendence.

On Conjectures

Cusanus's second great work, *On Conjectures* (*De coniecturis*, ca. 1443), contains his working out of the clarification summarized above. Continuing the age-old platonic tradition that goes back ultimately to Plato's *Timaeus,* Nicholas divides being into four levels: God, intelligence, soul, and body. He constructs his metaphysics of oneness, or unity, on this foundation.

Each level represents one region of the unified whole. Again Nicholas calls on a symbol, this time that of numbers along with that of figures. All numbers are "enfolded" in the number one. Through "unfolding" in the sequence 1, 2, 3, and 4, the plural number 10 comes about as the sum of the quaternary, while the ternary is the symbol of the Trinity and of true "enfolding." The number 10 is the root for the geometric sequence 10^2 and 10^3, that is, for further "unfolding" of the number to quadratic and cubic oneness. The numbers 1, 10, 100, and 1,000 are to serve as illustrations of the four levels of oneness, or unity.

One will recognize the fourth, physical level of oneness most clearly in the cubic element of the symbol sequence, while the third and second, in contrast, will be found only in strained correspondences. Only in the number one does a person see the principle of divine oneness represented satisfactorily. Yet more important is the fundamental concept common to all the symbols, according to which each level presents a unified whole in a diversity of expression. With this Cusanus, who by means of the concept of oneness brings together God, intelligences, souls, and bodies into a whole, becomes, after John Scotus Eriugena (ca. 800–ca. 877), the great thinker of the Middle Ages.

This symbolic metaphysics of oneness protects Nicholas from the monisitic dangers into which it was possible for the metaphysics of being in the *Learned Ignorance* to lead him. In addition, it sets him on a path toward understanding the essence of things better than do all other points of departure that start out with number symbolism. If oneness descends from its lofty heights it becomes otherness or differentiation to ever increasing degrees. Every number except the number one is oneness through the addition of differentiation to oneness. In this way every oneness is part of the higher oneness. Here Nicholas achieves a deepened view of the neoplatonic hierarchy by going beyond Pseudo-Dionysius, above all by working out the continuity of the path from oneness to differentiation and back again.

Four regions of the method of knowing correspond to the four unities. With my mind I grasp the essence of only those objects that owe their existence to my mind, such as logical and mathematical constructions. The essence of the real things is hidden from me since these things exist on another level of oneness. I can at most perceive them in a sensorial way—that is, with the organ that corresponds to their level—but only the one who created them can comprehend them. Therefore, all knowledge outside of logical-mathematical knowledge is only "conjecture." This view amounts to drawing a line of separation between being and knowing. This separation turns things into something "other," and thereby takes the first step toward separating the metaphysics of oneness from the metaphysics of being.

This separation becomes evident in the clear explanation of the concept of the "coincidence of opposites" (*coincidentia oppositorum*). In the realm of the senses there is no negation because the differentiating "no" does not enter our understanding until the intellect comes into play. For the senses there is no principle of contradiction. In contrast, it is fully valid in the realm of intellect. Convergence occurs in the realm of reason. The idea, or concept, of number includes even and odd numbers. Affirmation and negation exist together. However, the realm of the concept is not touched by the intellect's ways of expression that work with the principle of contradiction. There is also no convergence in the region of absolute oneness. Oneness is elevated above affirmation and negation.

In his later work, *The Vision of God* (*De visione Dei*, 1453), Nicholas named the coincidence of opposites the "wall of paradise" behind which God dwells. As long as the principle of contradiction is considered to be the principle of being, denial of it does lead to the consequences for which Cusanus was reproached. He regards it, however, as the principle of discursive thinking, as the principle of recognition of the third region of unity, and by doing so he averts the metaphysical danger slumbering in the denial of contradiction.

Enfolding and Unfolding

Learned Ignorance concluded with the instructive, yet unsatisfying recognition of not knowing, whose whole tendency is to point beyond itself. *On Conjectures* investigates the possibilities and conditions of positive statements. Common to both works—to Cusanus's entire thought—is the question about origin. As a part of this, his reflections on the very act of questioning are developing without being noticed. This self-questioning by the understanding mind grants Cusanus's thinking a significant place in the history of European philosophy. Certainly the insight that *Conjectures* achieves is, in the end, a tempered, humble, modest position. It is an acceptance of reality, not trying to pass over it, but trying to master it, pursuing knowledge with an earnestness that defines even a genius's sense of responsibility.

Conjectures is perhaps the most philosophical work of Cusanus, while *Learned Ignorance*—above all its third book—delves deeply into belief. The triad is already obvious in its structure. Book I is about the greatest per se, that which is the maximum absolute (*maximum absolutum*), God. Book II treats what is the greatest within certain limitations, the contracted maximum (*maximum contractum*), the world; and Book III discusses the absolute and contracted maximum (*maximum absolutum et contractum*), the redeemer as God and human.

Some have wanted to see in Nicholas the first thinker to break through the confines of the medieval view of the world, and they place him at the beginning of the modern view that looks out at the seemingly endless horizons of the natural sciences. This quasi-infinity did not disclose itself to him primarily through scientific experience, but rather through philosophical-theological speculation. If God enfolds everything in himself and the world is only the unfolding of God (*complicatio-explicatio*), then the world is a kind of second god, and, accordingly, infinite in a certain way. The fact that this infinity is only limitlessness, not infinity in its actual sense, needs no explanation. Since God unfolds himself, he and the finite are the same. Yet it is a sameness in otherness, or difference. It is potentially infinite in relation to space and time, but not actually infinite like God. It is, like God, a unity, or oneness, but only the circumscribed oneness of infinite possibilities.

The proof of a limitless world was momentous enough for the history of scholarly investigation. The Middle Ages conceived of the cosmos as a system of spherical surfaces with the earth in the center. Now this conception burst open into a system that knew neither above nor below, no poles, no center. While Cusanus did not give up the hierarchical thinking that posited for the cosmos a rank order of higher and lower spheres of more and less worth, he infused this thinking with an appreciation for the individual value of discrete things, each of which represents the whole. Although each thing is different from every other thing, the universe is still present in each and "contracts" itself into the respective individuality of each one. Since there is nothing real that is not different from all other real things there exists a general dissimilarity of things. Yet, since the oneness of the world is in them, they still correspond to each other. Dissimilarity and correspondence, *differentia* and *concordantia,* constitute the principles of the structure of the world. Nicholas never tires of looking for them in all areas. His future-oriented way of thinking in which the representation of the world becomes a reality in each individual entity anticipates the infinity that will manifest itself two centuries later in the monad of Leibniz's system.

The human being, too, illustrates this infinity. Through the capacities of the senses, understanding, and reasoning powers the human being comprehends things, at least in a conjectural way, and is therefore a microcosm, a human world. As a unit constituted in this way a person is a human god. However, if the world no longer has a firm point of reference, is not the human being in danger of getting lost in this boundless ocean?

At this juncture Cusanus introduces the aspect of his anthropology that points toward redemption. The human being does not founder in this world but exists above it, between heaven and earth, as nothing less than a human god. The quintessential "mediator," the divine redeemer, represents this middle point in a unique way. Cusanus's Christology becomes the foundation of his anthropology. Christ is always the model for the human being, not only morally, as perhaps the superficial pastoral interpretations of his example might suggest, but in relation to the person's entire being. Christology is capable of leading to the deciphering of the entire human being. Given his divinity and humanity Christ is the unified combination of everything. In one of his final sermons Nicholas expressed it this way: "Whatever intellectually gifted people are capable of knowing was reality in Christ." Christ possessed every perfection attainable by humans. In his greatness he enfolded in actuality everything that is possible in the realm of that which is contracted.

Unity and Multiplicity

The hastiness with which our survey must skim over Cusanus's works prevents us from mentioning even briefly the wealth of thought that, beginning with *Learned Ignorance,* he elaborated in treatises, dialogues, and sermons, applying himself to the task again and again for over two decades. His reflection *On the Origin* (*De principio*), written in 1459, offers perhaps the easiest access to his metaphysical speculation. God, he stresses here once again, exists above the realm of being. The source of things is not one of the things that have a source. Compared to creation he is nonbeing, while seen as the source he is being to the highest degree. In repeated attempts Cusanus explains the participation of that which is in the greatness of God, and using primarily triadic equivalents he reveals how they correspond to each other. Oneness, unity (*unitas*) belongs to the Father, equality (*aequalitas*) to the Son, connection (*connectio*) to the Holy Spirit. Correspondingly creatures unfold themselves in multiplicity (*pluralitas*), diversity (*diversitas*), and differentiation (*distinctio*).

Let us cite here, as an example, only Nicholas's sermon on the Lord's Prayer that has come down to us in the Mosel-Franconian dialect. The sermon goes into these interrelated concepts in an illuminating way and reveals in its affinity to *Learned Ignorance* the more than theoretical significance that Cusanus ascribed to his insights. He considered them universally applicable as a guide (*manuductio*) for believers and, ultimately also for unbelievers. In the logical extension of the principles to unbelievers, he declared his absolute trust in the value of Christian doctrine defined in such a way that its universality goes beyond the limits of a creed.

Nicholas regarded his perceptions to be universally applicable also in the sense of being universally understandable. They had to be comprehensible to the layperson, too, for as a human being, the layperson possesses infinite possibilities just as well as the learned philosopher. In *The Layperson* (*Idiota*) Cusanus leads a Roman spooncarver, drawing on the carver's craft as the starting point, from an understanding of the concept of the spoon all the way to the perception of deep relationships. Cusanus gradually reveals these by helpfully guiding the spooncarver in conversation. In this way the philosopher fulfilled the task assigned to him of being a divine co-creator. He did this by developing the possibilities of thought in his fellow human being.

Cusanus considered it easy to lead people to understanding. This guidance ought to work even at play. When the young sons of the Duke of Bavaria visited Nicholas in Rome he entertained them with a new game. In *The Game of Spheres* (*De ludo globi*) he reports on his conversation with the boys about the symbolic meaning of how they threw the balls. The boys, carried away by the surprising new knowledge, forgot about the game as the conversation led them on in their thinking. Nothing demonstrates more strikingly how far this kind of education was removed from the schoolbook learning of the day.

Hercules of the Eugenians

We have been carried up to the heights of philosophical speculation, but in doing so we have almost forgotten that once again our thinker was getting involved in the affairs of the day. The year 1437 was, on the one hand, the year of his great revelation. On the other hand, it was the year when the success at Constantinople placed him at the forefront of European politicians. From now on he is active in the great events of the world. We will follow him in this activity, astonished at the energy with which he pursues politics, while at the same time performing pastoral care, preaching, taking care of his ever-expanding assets, and writing, one after another, philosophical and theological works that reach into the uttermost depths of human understanding.

Nicholas was able to participate for only a short time in the council's work that on July 5, 1439, led to union with the Greeks—only a temporary union, of course. More urgent for Pope Eugenius IV was the disagreement with the council fathers who continued to meet in Basel. This struggle turned into a contest for support in European Christendom. The stance of the German nation was of great significance. At the electoral session in Frankfurt on March 17, 1438, the German electors combined their choice of the new king, Albert II, with their declaration of neutrality toward Eugenius IV and the Council of Basel. The king sided with them. It would take a full ten years of endless negotiations to break the German neutrality and draw the princes to the side of the pope. The sharpest minds were sent to Germany. Those who were prominent among them were Cardinal Albergati, Thomas Parentucelli, who became pope in 1447, John Carvajal, a Spaniard burning with desire for action, who as papal legate took on the hardships of foreign countries until the end of his life, and Torquemada, a cardinal since 1439 and one of the century's leading theologians.

The lone German among these influential nuncios was Nicholas of Cusa. Unlike the others who all dropped out over the course of the years, he remained involved from beginning to end. The fact that he appeared in the group of foreigners spelled great danger for his reputation in Germany. People denounced him as a traitor and turncoat. Aeneas Sylvius called him the "Hercules of the Eugenians." As late as 1538 the zealous reformer, Johannes Kymeus, still disparaged Nicholas as "the pope's Hercules against the Germans." The title page of Kymeus's manuscript portrays Nicholas holding the cross of the redeemer toward the Germans who are kneeling before him, while the pope and cardinals, grasping the cord of his cardinal's hat, are pulling him over to the Roman camp. This illustration alludes to the compensation Cusanus received for his papal service. Perhaps another factor was his countrymen's jealousy over the advancement of this man from the Mosel in service to the Curia. As a way of characterizing the unusual nature of his career, people compared the German cardinal to a white raven.

If we evaluate prudently what motivated him to rescue the German nation for the Roman Church we will attribute as much to his ambition as to his sense of responsibility.

Disputes with the Council of Basel

The first papal legation sent to break the neutrality of the Germans was dispatched from Ferrara on September 15, 1438, in order to be at the imperial diet in Nuremberg scheduled for October. Cusanus's name is included in the list of those designated by the pope, but Nicholas himself had already been back in Germany for some time. On June 6, 1438, Eugenius IV had sent him with a letter to the Swabian imperial cities in which he summoned them to a hearing that was supposed to help prevent the threatening schism. Another mission that demonstrates clearly the importance Nicholas had gained on the political stage was the one from the poet-king René of Anjou, Duke of Lorraine. On July 24, 1438, in Capua near Naples he empowered Nicholas, along with Jacob von Sierck and three magnates from Lorraine to appear before the German royal couple and relinquish his claims—inherited through Queen Johanna II—to the kingdoms of Hungary, Dalmatia, Croatia, Galicia, Lodomeria, Comania, and Bulgaria. During this same period Nicholas was already involved in negotiations in Southern Germany. Based on a Nuremberg city financial record, it appears that he was at an imperial diet in Nuremberg participating in discussions about preparations for the October diet, even though he was not the specifically designated papal representative.

At the Nuremberg imperial diet Nicholas fell into a dispute with Thomas of Courcelles, the legate of the Council of Basel. Nicholas pointed out the split in the council, which, he said, was already enough to raise doubts about the council's infallibility. The trump card he played was the decision of the Greeks to side with the minority—in the meantime it had become a convincing majority—that was united with the pope. Beyond this he underscored both the clear possibility that the council could err, and the right of the pope to change council decisions. Such talk might well have been surprising to listeners who had witnessed him only a few years earlier in Basel without, of course, paying close attention to his words.

The council's historian, John of Segovia, has passed along another, yet totally different, argument by Cusanus against the Council of Basel. Cusanus reportedly said in Nuremberg that nothing good could come out of Basel because the council stood under an unfavorable alignment of the stars. Six years later in 1444 he took advantage of being in Nuremberg for an imperial diet in order to purchase, along with numerous books, a celestial globe, an astrolabe, and a turquet. These were valuable astronomical instruments that had been in the possession of the Bohemian royal house.

From the imperial diet in Nuremberg Nicholas turned to Münstermaifeld. There, on December 1, 1438, he participated as provost in the regular renewal of contracts with the tenants in the provostship. He left behind notes, written in his own hand, about the negotiations. It was important for him to be present in his benefices at this particular time. The Council of Basel had taken the benefices away from the traitor, and on March 26, 1438, had already assigned the provostship of Münstermaifeld to the council auditor, John of Hungary. Other transfers followed. Proceedings that the Council of Basel had initiated against the legates of the minority on February 19, 1438, led to the declaration of complete privation on January 27, 1440. Anticipating this, Nicholas had taken defensive action with a papal bull of protection of December 21, 1438. In it the archdeacon of Hesbain, George Cesarini, along with two other dignitaries, were appointed to protect his benefices. The fact that the task was assigned to Cardinal Cesarini's brother shows how closely Nicholas was connected to the cardinal's entire family.

Yet any connections with the Curia would turn out to be useless wherever papal power could not assert itself. Thus, the weal
and woe of his Trier benefices depended on what the archbishop of
Trier thought. Jacob von Sierck succeeded Raban as archbishop in
1439. He was one of the most crafty, sly, and enterprising imperial
princes of his day. Recognizing the opportunities arising out of the
schism he, too, joined the neutral side. He saw no reason to take
action against Cusanus, through whom he could maintain contact
with the Curia, while at the same time Nicholas was still recognized as the confidant of powerful circles in the archbishopric.

Advocate and Negotiator

During the ten years Nicholas spent in Germany as papal legate he was occupied with numerous affairs of his homeland. In
some cases these were ecclesiastical tasks that the pope or legates
entrusted to him, among which the work of reform was prominent. In other cases he was approached by the nobility, middle-
class citizens, prelates, foundations, corporations, and institutions
of his homeland to mediate their disputes. Just to enumerate all
these activities would fill many pages! Let us content ourselves
with a few examples.

On September 6, 1438, the pope delegated Nicholas to install a
vicar in the parish church at Alf, in the jurisdiction of Zell, and on
December 29, 1439, authorized him to transfer the provostship of
Maria ad Gradus in Mainz to John of Lieser, advisor to the archbishop of Mainz. From May 1440 to September 1441 Nicholas was
busy integrating the parish church of St. Isidor outside Trier, which
had been devastated in the Manderscheid affair, into St. Catherine's
Convent. By the power of full apostolic authority he granted a
business partner of the Krebs family, the nobleman Gottfried von
Esch, free choice of a father confessor on February 22, 1441. In the
course of the same year Archbishop Jacob assigned him inspection

of the Trier collegiate churches, St. Simeon and St. Paulin. In September 1442, although he was no longer dean at St. Florin, he represented the rights of the church in its dispute with the parish and magistrates of Obermendig before a mediation panel composed of several of the noblemen in the chapter. On April 26, 1443, the pope entrusted Nicholas with the defense of the apostolic writer, Bartholomew de Monte, in his dispute with a canon at St. Peter's in Mainz. On April 30, 1443, he was present in Trier when Henry Greiffenclau zu Vollrad relinquished the cathedral deanery. On May 30, 1443, working together with Carvajal in Mainz Nicholas organized the Ordinary of the Mass at St. Simeon in Trier.

On the basis of the full authority the pope had conferred on him, Nicholas extended his activity further to convey ecclesiastical benefices in the Liège diocese. He had been active there since June 1443. On December 26, 1443, the pope gave him the task of annexing a benefice in Maria ad Gradus in Mainz to the provostship or to the related office of the sacristan. Later he placed the parish church at Kriftel under the authority of the chapter. On April 19 and 24, 1444 he is arbitrator in a dispute between the village priest in Löf near Münstermaifeld and St. Maximin's Cloister regarding the rights to levy tithes in Mörz and Löf. On April 22, 1444, at the request of two knights, Stifart Walpod von Bassenheim and Friedrich vom Stein, he arranged a settlement in their dispute about the income of Friedrich's wife, who was a daughter of the Bassenheimers. On August 28, 1444, Eugenius IV delegated Nicholas to install the papal **abbreviator**, Johannes Gryssgin, as vicar in Boppard, and on December 30, 1444, to install Heinrich Gebuer into a prebendary at Maria ad Gradus in Mainz.

Negotiations to settle a dispute between Archbishop Jacob and the Canon Adam Foyl of Irmentraut dragged on from August 1445 until February 1446. The conflict had developed when a faction of several members of the chapter opposed unauthorized actions of the archbishop. In the end Nicholas, who defended the canon, drafted in his own hand the depositions that led to the settlement.

On March 7, 1446, the pope instructed the new bishop of Worms to deliver into Cusanus's hands an oath of allegiance to the Apostolic See. At the end of 1448 Nicholas, on behalf of Carvajal, cleared up the misgivings of the Cistercian nuns in Gräfenthal on the Lower Rhine about maintaining the vow of poverty. On January 1, 1449, Carvajal appointed Nicholas to investigate the incorporation of the diocese of St. Simeon in Trier into deanery and chapter. On May 2, 1449, Nicholas, no longer provost of Münstermaifeld, endorsed the new statutes of the church after a thorough examination on behalf of the papal legate. He was substantially involved in the reform of the Springiersbach Cloister that had been mandated on July 23, 1449. At the same time he once again intervened in the disagreement between of the archbishop of Trier with the rebellious canons. On the one hand, the conflict was intertwined with tensions between the clergy and citizens of Trier, but on the other hand, it had wider political dimensions as a result of Burgundian influence. On October 24, 1449, the pope instructed Cusanus to take sharp measures against the defiant canons.

During these years Cusanus often returned to the Mosel, whether to Koblenz, where, after he had relinquished the title of dean in 1439, he still kept a residence as canon of St. Florin, whether to Münstermaifeld, or to Kues. However, this contact with the region where he grew up changed radically when he went to Rome at the end of 1449. Kues saw him only one more time as he passed by while in the Mosel region on his legation journey of 1451. Later, events in the Tyrol prevented him from making the trip home that he had planned for the spring of 1460. Eventually only his heart returned home, for it was buried in Kues.

Still, not only love kept him attached to his home, but also various responsibilities, one of which was the hospital rising on its

FIGURE 5. Bernkastel-Kues today. Kues is seen on the left side of the Mosel River, with St. Nicholas Hospital near the water, to the right of the bridge.

construction site. Again and again his friends in the nobility turned to him when they needed help. For example, on November 1, 1451, he secured for Dietrich von Manderscheid through the Echtern-ach Cloister a suitable settlement for the right of presentation in Laufeld. On March 12, 1459 Count Gebhard von Sayn requested Pope Pius II to have Nicholas order the reform—the reform the Count was not able to bring about by himself—of his private mon-asteries, Marienstatt and Sayn. Particularly characteristic, however, is Cusanus's intercession in 1456 and 1457 with Pope Calixtus III on behalf of the agreement concluded by the Trier estates that put the choice of the archbishop in the hands of the nobility. Here we see that Nicholas's thinking in regard to his estimation of the rights of the laity, understood in terms of rank, was scarcely different than it had been thirty years earlier when he, as chancellor for Ulrich, who was elected by the estates, defended the principle of the laity. He took this position in 1456 at a time when he himself, as head of the chapter, had come into sharp conflict with lay authority. But more about this later!

A Breathtaking Schedule

In the 1440s the scenes of Nicholas's struggle for the unity of the church were the great assemblies of the German princes and cities. Their interplay of interests, their back and forth, the often very personal discussions in which the issue of the church's structure was debated from every point of view, the great speeches and the more than exhaustive treatises by Cusanus himself—all of this alone would fill a book. Let us content ourselves with a listing of the meeting places.

We first see Nicholas in March and April of 1439 at the congress of princes in Mainz. Legates of the kings of England and France were also in attendance. At first Nicholas spent the time in Mainz without any assignment. On April 16 the papal legates arrived, and the pope added Nicholas to them. Then the negotiations were moved to Basel. What was left of the minority tried in vain to avert the schism that the council initiated on June 25 by removing Eugenius IV.

Once again Nicholas was at the scene of action when he went to the electoral diet held in Frankfurt in August. This was a time when the council was trying to win over the German princes. Shortly before this, Nicholas had conferred in Koblenz with John of Gelnhausen, the **abbot** of Maulbronn, along with John of Lieser and Tilmann of Linz, representatives of the electors of the Palatinate, Mainz and Cologne. Nicholas was trying to induce them to side with Eugenius IV. The council called upon the princes gathered in Frankfurt to arrest Cusanus, but to no avail.

Nicholas was also present at the ensuing provincial council in Mainz at the end of August. We find him in Mainz in the following months as well, certainly on November 8 when he provided a detailed memorandum for a legate who would represent the king at the Frankfurt diet of princes in November 1439. The memorandum called for breaking off relationships with Basel and siding unambiguously with Eugenius. On December 19, 1439, Nicholas was in Koblenz, where he exchanged the deanery of St. Florin for other small benefices. On the following day he and the second papal legate, Jacob de Oratoribus, were at the electoral diet in Lahnstein, where they presented anew the arguments in support of Eugenius. On February 12, 1440, while in Kues, he completed *On Learned Ignorance.*

What a breathtaking pace! We would have to trace Nicholas's performance for decades, even years, in order to comprehend the unique achievement it represents.

Conflict and Triumph

After only one year's rule King Albert died on October 27, 1439, and his successor was to be chosen at an electoral diet in Frankfurt. Naturally, the outcome would be important for the nation's relationship to pope and council. Thus, on January 10, 1440, Eugenius IV gave detailed instructions regarding the diet to his two legates, Nicholas of Cusa and Jacob de Oratoribus. In accordance with their charge the legates stayed in the background during the election itself, but afterwards approached the electors with a specific request. The electors retreated behind the argument that they could not make any decision without the new king. The king was Frederick III, Duke of Austria, whose reign of over fifty years has gone down in German history as an epoch of a largely absent king.

The issue about the church—the conflict between pope and council—dragged on without a decision throughout 1440. The imperial diet of Nuremberg, initially scheduled for November 30, was postponed until January 6, 1441, and then cancelled altogether. Consequently, the next imperial gathering was not held until February in Mainz. It lasted until April. Nicholas had tried to draw Jacob von Sierck over to the side of the pope. He delivered Eugenius's message to Jacob that the pope was canceling the 10,000 florin tax, known as the **servitia**, that Jacob, as new archbishop, would otherwise have to send to Rome. Two years later Jacob had the antipope in Basel, Felix V, pay him the same amount for his services in arranging a marriage for a two-year-old granddaughter of the antipope. In Mainz, little impressed by the pope's tax forgiveness, Jacob let the council's legate, Cardinal Louis Aleman, be the honorary chair. Aleman, and after him Thomas of Courcelles, made a deep impression on the gathering with their remarks. Even greater was Cusanus's success when he struck back with a counter-speech on the following day. A rejoinder three days later by John of Segovia was scarcely able to diminish its effect. It should be noted that ten years later, in December 1454, Nicholas and Segovia—and this testifies to the breadth of their horizons—entered into a more peaceful discussion on the totally different topic of the holy Trinity and presentation of this theme to the Muslims.

In Mainz no one could yet feel like the victor, but a slight tendency in Eugenius's favor was apparent. Nevertheless, for the papal legates this was only the beginning. An imperial diet was scheduled for November 11, 1441, in Frankfurt. Nicholas had already arrived before November 7. The diet was poorly attended and achieved no significant progress. An additional imperial diet held in Frankfurt from the end of May until the middle of August 1442 turned out to be a setback for Nicholas and the papal legates since the king chose to continue the policy of neutrality.

Two speeches stand at the center of the debate about the church. One was by the council's legate, Cardinal Nicholas de Tu-

deschis, the well-known canonist who went by the name of Pan-
ormitanus in the history of canon law. He held forth from June 14
to 18. The other was by Cusanus who spoke for an additional three
days, from June 21 to 23. The record of these expositions covers
a full 130 quarto pages, even though Cusanus's speech was written down after the fact and certainly represents an abridgment of
what he said. Grouped around these two presentations are numerous smaller replies, rejoinders, rejoinders to rejoinders, endless
treatises, and contributions to the discussion that set forth the opposing viewpoints again and again.

Some have wondered whether such activity might have had little bearing on the actual political decisions. Many of the very same
points were repeated over and over. No doubt what was important
was not the strength of one's argument but one's appearance before the conference. Cusanus was subject to this pressure, too, and
repeated himself. Nevertheless, in his case there is a certain something that impresses us again and again, not the least of which is
that little extra in his expositions, which, though often slight, is
something his opponents could not muster.

An example of this is the *Dialogue against the Amadeists* (*Dialo-
gus concludens Amedistarum errorem*) that Cusanus composed on the
occasion of the Mainz conference of 1441. The work is especially
illustrative of how he constructs his position. He aims to demonstrate, as the title indicates, the aberration of the Amadeists—the
followers of the Basel pope, the former Duke Amadeus of Savoy—by citing their own actions and doctrinal pronouncements at
the Council of Basel. The central question was, what is the correct
view of the council? According to Cusanus the Council of Basel
specifically gave the pope, as "head of the church" and "head of
the council" the leading role in representing the entire church.

Yet the opponents did not give up. Year after year, from diet to
diet the mountain of records piled up higher and higher—records

from February 1443, from November 1443 until January 1444, and from August until October 1444, each time in Nuremberg; then in June 1445, and in September and October of 1446 in Frankfurt. Carvajal and Cusanus are the crucial personalities in these later years. Finally, at the diet at Aschaffenburg in July 1447 their efforts created the conditions for the German princes to side with the Roman pope. The arrangements worked out with the Curia resulted in a **concordat** between the Apostolic See and the German Nation. This "Concordat of Vienna," concluded in that city on February 17, 1448, governed relations between the Holy Roman Empire and the Curia until the end of the empire.

Carvajal was already rewarded with the red cardinal's hat in 1446. Eugenius IV intended to appoint Nicholas of Cusa, too, but the pope died before announcing the distinction. In 1447 Thomas Parentucelli, Cusanus's friend of many years, became the new pope under the name of Nicholas V. On December 20, 1448, he publicly elevated the German to cardinal, and on January 3, 1449, assigned him St. Peter in Chains (*San Pietro in Vincoli*) as his **titular church**. From then on the Italians would call him the "Cardinal of St. Peter." Yet shortly before this he attained the distinction with perhaps the highest virtue when, at the conclave from which Parentucelli emerged as the victor, Nicholas also received votes during the process. Nothing bears better witness to the respect that he enjoyed in the church.

The Power of the Pope

To what extent did Cusanus's views about the church change during these years, and to what extent did they stay the same? Two of his letters provide an answer. One was to a Carthusian monastery at the beginning of 1441, and one to the Castilian, Rodrigo Sánchez de Arévalo in May 1442. In essence one cannot speak of him going over to the pope when he merely followed a consistent path, since only conformity with the Roman Church assured him, even in his Basel years, of the infallibility promised to the church. However, the two letters also show how within this context he gives increasing emphasis to the power of the pope. To the extent that, based on the promise to Peter, one can speak of an absolute power in the church, this power belongs to the pope as "holy prince" (*sacer princeps*). In the first letter he still differentiates between the Apostolic See and the person of the pope. In the letter to Rodrigo he dispenses with the differentiation. Concentrating the infallibility in the person of the pope is unthinkable without the insight into the relationship between enfolding and unfolding that he had gained in *Learned Ignorance*. In *The Catholic Concordance* the pope represented the church only vaguely, in a "muddled" way. Now Cusanus sees the entire church enfolded in him, and it unfolds itself to its full extent through the succession of hierarchical ranks. In this fundamental turnabout, to a viewpoint from the top down, we recognize the essential difference. The consequences for the relationship between pope and council follow inevitably.

The factor that remained constant through all of this was Cusanus's underlying endeavor to achieve a unity that encompasses both concepts. This effort was fueled not least by the experience of this man of thought in the strife of his time. He came to see the Council of Basel as the last failed attempt to build unity from the bottom up. The great issues of the day were smothered by wrangling in the committees. Those wielding political power took the reins of history into their hands. Despite this Cusanus never completely gave up the concept of the council because he was aware of the significance of the unfolded creation just as much as he was aware of God's greatness that was revealed in this creation. Bishops and believers also contribute to the construction of God's house. They contain, as it were, partial aspects of the eternal picture. For this reason, until the end of his life he supported the calling of councils because this carried out in the realm of the church what he understood by "universal."

Friends and Associates

In his activity at the imperial assemblies Nicholas initially held only the lower ranks of **papal orator** and **nuncio**. Not until July 22, 1446, did he receive the highest powers belonging to an apostolic legate. This gave him greater authority for the tasks the pope entrusted to him that went beyond the negotiations. Above all, by virtue of his full power of papal authority received on February 5, 1446, he was able to dispense numerous ecclesiastical privileges. These included the reinstatement of excommunicated clergy, the permission of free choice of a father confessor, the dispensation from a stigma of birth, dispensation from marriage, the exchange of benefices, absolution from defilement of a nun, approval of portable altars, the permission for clerics to be certified, etc., etc. In the work of salvation this was mundane, but each favor was of the greatest importance to the one who received it!

Each decision—250 uses of full power are laid down numerically in the papal bulls—was accompanied by investigations, deliberations, and, not least of all, written work. People have criticized Cusanus not only for chasing after benefices for himself, but also for the attention he paid to the livelihood of those who assisted him. After an objective look at the reality of Cusanus's daily life with its abundance of tasks one would have to concede that he needed the staff to carry out these duties.

Here we can name only a few of his helpers: Wigand von Homberg, Johann von Bastogne, Peter von Erkelenz, Walther von Gouda, Johannes Stam the Elder, and the Younger, and Heinrich Pomert. For a time even a bishop, the Scotsman Thomas Livingston, to whom the Council of Basel had transferred the Dunkeld diocese, accompanied him as an assistant. We could present the life of each one of them in a separate biography. A number of them held influential positions in the church. From the papal registers alone we can identify approximately fifty associates of whom no doubt one third were permanent members of his household. Of course, with these numbers he still ranked far behind most of his fellow cardinals.

Through his immense, increasing number of tasks Nicholas came in contact with the leading society of his day. There were the royal houses—the Wittelsbachs in the many branches of their line; the Brandenburgers with their hero, Albert Achilles; the House of Austria that provided the emperor; and Philip, the "Grand Duke" of Burgundy. What satisfaction it was for a son of the middle class now as a cardinal to rank at the same societal level as they. He was regarded as highly as a prince of the blood.

In addition, he came in contact with circles of those in the arts and science as well as circles of the devout. A special friendship bound him to the monks of Tegernsee. He even reserved a cell there for use in his old age. The correspondence he maintained with the monks in the 1450s plumbs the depths of theological-philosophical understanding. To the abbot, Kaspar Aindorffer, he explained once more the meaning of his doctrine of coincidence. By means of the darkness of reason we receive only negative knowledge about God. Thus God is in danger of becoming nothing. We must go one step further to the place where there is neither positive nor negative. God is precisely there.

Nicholas was also in close touch with the Carthusians who offered a much-praised model for the orders of their day. As at Tegernesee Nicholas looked forward to a place reserved in the Carthusian monastery at Koblenz for his old age. In Mainz Marcellus Geist transmitted Cusanus's works. Denys (Dionysius) the Carthusian was closely connected with Nicholas. The prior of the Carthusian monastery in Koblenz became supervisor of the Nicholas

Hospital. Through Cusanus's effort the Carthusians secured ownership in 1448 of larger holdings near the Rhine and in the Netherlands.

A Cusanus circle formed in Aachen. Its intellectual leader was the doctor, Johannes Scoblant. He belonged to the Louvain circle of scholars, and Cusanus sent him his newly written mathematical treatises to be copied. Two hundred and fifty years later this copy came into the hands of the famous mathematician, John Wallis, who relied on it in his correspondence with Leibniz about cycloids.

At the time Germany certainly knew of no other personality than Cusanus who, in every region of the country, gained such self-evident respect in the influential circles of politics, academic disciplines, and the church. In addition, the harshness with which his opponents attacked him testifies to their recognition of his significance, even if they dreaded him.

Administrator and Author

Nicholas had far outgrown the Mosel region. This outward movement is reflected also in the expansion of what he possessed, particularly in the Netherlands. An important facet we come across in his benefice dealings is the circle of friends who were ready to help him, who occupied themselves with his writing, promoted it by making copies, and handed it down to posterity.

On April 16, 1438, he received a cathedral prebend in Liège, and on February 21, 1443, in Utrecht. In the summer of 1443 he acquired the Schindel parish in Brabant. By 1441 he had already reached an agreement with Philip, brother of the Archbishop Jacob von Sierck, to exchange the provostship of Münstermaifeld for the archdiaconate of Brabant in the Liège diocese. On September 13, 1445, he was admitted to the position of archdeacon, and for several years after this he referred to himself with this highest-ranking title. In addition to this distinction he received the provostship of

Oldenzaal no later than 1446, and in his homeland he acquired the parish church of St. Wendel.

The new benefices in the Netherlands frequently compelled Cusanus to spend time there. Moreover, as archdeacon he had to fulfill numerous duties of official church administration. It is doubtful, however, whether he was always adept at this, judging from the complaints against a number of his actions. On the other hand, his new locations of activity led him into the influential political world of the Netherlands. So it is that we see him engaged in resolving a dispute between Walram von Moers and Rudolf von Diepholz about the bishopric of Utrecht. One benefit we gain from Nicholas's scholarly works is that they identify the locations of his activity. For example, he was in Liège on March 2, 1447, when he completed his dialogue, *On the Origin of All Things* (*De genesi*).

This work directs our attention back to Nicholas's unabated activity in the service of knowledge. His great works—*Learned Ignorance,* that received its *Apology* in 1449 in response to attacks by Johannes Wenck, and the *Conjectures*—were joined by several small treatises: prior to 1445 the dialogue *On the Hidden God* (*De Deo abscondito*); at the beginning of 1445 the treatise *On the Search for God* (*De quaerendo Deum*); a few months later the work *On Being a Son of God* (*De filiatione Dei*); probably around the beginning of 1446, relating to a verse in the Epistle of James, *On the Gift of the Father of Light* (*De dato patris luminum*); and finally in 1447 *On the Origin of All Things*. Even the titles point towards the theme that Nicholas investigated with ever-new approaches, but whose essence was never to be entirely revealed: the mystery of God and the world. He attempted to follow two paths to understanding: the path of "conjecture," and the path of the "search for God," one philosophical, the other theological. One group of the works is indebted to the former path, another group to the latter. Both groups demonstrate anew the tension that pervades his thought, while they testify no less to the multitude of perspectives from which Nicholas looked at the question of being.

First Year as a Cardinal

On January 11, 1450, Pope Nicholas V placed the red hat on the new cardinal, and eight days later his mouth was opened symbolically. With these actions he was made a full member of the highest governing body of the Roman Church, the same body that, joined with the pope, Cusanus himself had identified as having the highest representative function for the Christian world.

The year 1450 was a time of celebration for Rome. The pope, dividing the century in half, declared 1450 a **Jubilee Year**, and this drew into the Eternal City innumerable pilgrims who desired to obtain the Jubilee Indulgence. For Cusanus it was a year of rest and reflection, a year lived at a slower pace. In the summer, he, like his papal friend, traveled to Abruzzi. Here he applied himself to his great work The Layperson (Idiota, 1450), which he divided into four books: On Wisdom (De sapientia) I and II; On the Mind (De mente); and On Experiments with Scales (De staticis experimentis). The four follow a path from theology through epistemology to natural philosophy.

Additional works dealt with questions of mathematics and geometry without Nicholas ever losing sight of the symbolic meaning of number and figure. He pursued this kind of investigation until the end of his life. In his book On the Squaring of the Circle (De quadratura circuli, 1458) he struggled hopelessly in a fruitless effort to solve a problem that was to engage many minds in an unproductive pursuit.

The fourth book of The Layperson represents Cusanus's significance in the history of the natural sciences, in that the book's epigrammatic title cites "experiments," pointing to experience gained by means of experimenting with scales. In so doing he made the

FIGURE 6. One of the earliest images of Cusanus: "Nicolaus von cusa cardinal," shown with the cardinal's (red) hat in the *Nuremberg Chronicle* of 1493, an illustrated history of the world also known as *Schedel's World Chronicle*.

transition from investigating qualitative character to measuring quantitative size; that is, he moved from the medieval philosophy of nature to modern natural science. He immediately applied the process of quantitative measurement to medicine, and indicated the possibilities that lay in determining the specific gravity of blood and urine and in determining pulse and breathing rates. He explained the meaning of, and procedure for, measuring humidity, and how one had to pay attention to specific gravity when casting bells and cannon. It is uncertain to what extent Cusanus should be characterized as a pioneer of modern natural science, but he knew he was on the verge of unlimited possibilities for new understanding, though he was not yet able to predict the broad sweep of their tangible forms.

The Nature of the German Legation

Given his deep understanding of the state of the church, of its defects and perils, Cusanus was unable to adhere to a leisurely pace of life. He was of the view that the settlement of the schism provided by no means a definitive solution to the problems of the church. Any successes would remain superficial if the church did not set moral standards and reform ecclesiastical life. Out of love for his fatherland Cusanus wanted to renew his country from the ground up, and on December 24, 1450, the pope appointed him, as he wished, legate. Now Cusanus himself was to pronounce the favor of the Jubilee Indulgence on any of those in Germany who had been hindered in making the pilgrimage to Rome.

Indulgences have acquired a bad name because of their misuse. How could monetary offerings substitute for the true spirit of repentance? Today when we view the pre-Reformation era objectively we are less judgmental about the interweaving of the earthly and heavenly and about the human shortcomings that give rise in one century to a distortion like indulgences, and in another century to perhaps even worse practices.

Nicholas of Cusa, believing in the spiritual power of indulgences, and convinced that they could reduce the punishment for one's sins, viewed his legation first and foremost as a pastoral assignment. There was scarcely a place where he did not step into the pulpit! His sermons reveal how far he distanced himself from the superficial religiosity that people so quickly connect with indulgences. In fact, he specifically opposed all forms of outward expression of faith that lacked inward conviction. He placed faith and sacrament at the center of his appeal to the conscience of his contemporaries. Freeing the core and essence of Christian faith from the jumbled, rampant, wild growth of medieval requirements, he turned attention above all to the sacrament of the Eucharist. He saw all other sacraments enfolded in it as the sacrament of sacraments, for Christ, the only agent of saving grace, is present in it.

At the same time he tried vigorously to eliminate whatever was superfluous since, as such, it was potentially harmful. He forbade, for example, the veneration of the sacred blood at Wilsnack, fought the trade in fraudulent relics, and opposed the excessive number of feast days. In order that the fundamentals of the faith could be conveyed to the people he had panels hung in churches on which the Lord's Prayer, the Hail Mary, the Apostles' Creed, and the Ten Commandments were inscribed.

Cusanus's sermons calling urgently for repentance had to fall on deaf ears when listeners were not ready for the call. If persuasion did not bring about repentance then one would have to arouse it by means of pain caused by whatever force the kingdom of heaven can tolerate. After all, of the numerous full powers of authority that the pope granted Cusanus the centerpiece was his assignment to reform the German church. While archbishops and bishops were exempted from the legate's direct intervention for reform, he had complete freedom of action regarding other ecclesiastical officials. He could place people in, and remove them from, office, he could reduce their rank, and he could punish with penance, excommunication and interdict whomever, wherever, and whenever he wanted. Among the reform decrees he pronounced during his more than year-long journey the ones important for their practical effect were above all: the ban on concubines; the forbiddance of financial abuse in granting benefices; and the decrees initiating reform of the orders, on keeping nuns strictly enclosed within their cloisters, and stipulating dignified conduct at worship services.

The Route of the German Legation

Before Nicholas set out on his journey the pope favored him at the close of his curial year with yet another honor of a special sort by giving him permission to say Mass at the papal altar in Rome's Basilica of Saint Mary Major (*Santa Maria Maggiore*). This honor was bestowed only five times in the entire century. Then on the last day of 1450 Nicholas left the city to carry his message of reform to the North.

In a message that Cusanus had already sent ahead on December 8 he had requested the archbishop of Salzburg to call a provincial council for February 3 at which Cusanus, as legate, intended to take up the reform activity. He began his work in the empire itself on January 25, 1451, in Spittal on the Drava River when he called the Cistercian abbots of the Salzburg Province to a consultation in Wiener Neustadt.

His journey took him first of all to Salzburg, then down the Danube to Wiener Neustadt by way of Passau and back through Vienna, Melk, and Lambach to Salzburg. From here he set out for Bavaria. By way of Munich, Freising, and Eichstätt he reached Nuremberg, where he stayed for two weeks in April. Then he spent two weeks in Bamberg, another two in Würzburg, and after stops in Erfurt and Halle arrived in Magdeburg in June for a longer stay. After visiting Halberstadt, Wolfenbüttel, and Riddagshausen his next extended stay was in Hildesheim. At the end of July he traveled via Hannover, Minden, and Nordhorn to Deventer, from where he went to Diepenveen, the sister house of the Windesheim Congregation, and to Windesheim itself. The next destinations were Zwolle, Kampen, Utrecht, Amsterdam, the Egmond Benedictine Abbey, Haarlem, Rijnsburg, Leiden, and again Utrecht. From Arnhem his course took him through Nimwegen, Roermond, and Heinsberg to Maastricht. After a detour to Aachen his trip continued through Sint Truiden, Hasselt and Tongern, Liège, and Malmedy to Trier where he stayed for two weeks at the end of October and the beginning of November.

Then the journey resumed its brisk prace. The only part of the course we know for sure is that he was in Kues on November 9. By November 13 he was already in Mainz. At the beginning of December he left Mainz to go down the Rhine again, spent Christmas in Cologne, and in quick succession went to Aachen, Maastricht, Hasselt, Louvain, and Brussels, where at the end of January he met Philip of Burgundy. He returned to Louvain and Maastricht, and in March, after another stay in Cologne, pressed southward. Going through Koblenz, Frankfurt, Aschaffenburg, Heilbronn, and Munich he arrived in his Brixen diocese at the end of March or the beginning of April 1451. This concluded the reform journey itself, although reform activity then continued in Brixen.

In the summer of 1452 Cusanus returned to Bavaria once more. After the hurried journey in which Cusanus had left his mark in the German territories, numerous matters required follow-up clarification. These matters included complaints, appeals to the pope against Cusanus's measures, and explanations that he himself had to present. All of this was to demand his attention again when in 1453 he was called to Rome to report on his work.

Reception of the Legate

Scarcely a single day of Cusanus's journey is undocumented, whether by ordinances, legal documents, indulgences, correspondence, sermons, or detailed reports of chroniclers! Whenever Cusanus entered a town—riding a donkey, like his Lord once did—people came in droves. They observed with great admiration his example of absolute modesty. Everywhere he went, towns and princes, clerics and laity gave him festive receptions. They spared nothing on food, drink, and décor. As was characteristic for the period, they tried to drown the problems of the day for at least a few moments in festivities that went to excess. There is scarcely an envoy's report about the deliberations at hand that forgets to mention the revelry!

Perhaps one reason why people celebrated the legate with great pomp was in order to divert his attention from more serious things. Liège provides an example. Its friendliness vanished abruptly when Cusanus took up his reforms. Later Cusanus reproached the people of Liège, saying that at first they gave him a splendid reception like the Jews gave Christ on Palm Sunday, but then they spurned him when he wanted to cleanse the temple.

Whenever Cusanus's message for reform met with opposition he could not bring himself to compromise. Instead he stood firm. Up to this point, we have come to know Cusanus as a skillful mediator, but here, when he stepped forth as an authority, a judge, a ruler, his inability to understand others revealed itself clearly. He knew this and regretted it. Yet he justified his position on the basis of his duty to carry out what he considered right, cost what it may. We find a peculiar divergence in how his contemporaries judged him. At first they accused Cusanus of betrayal and vacillation; later they called him thick-headed, inflexible, and narrow. They did not recognize that both characteristics were closely connected, that the inconsistencies of their age were represented in his person, and that the more painful struggle with these inconsistencies began within himself.

The Orders Resist Reform

The work of reform was meant to be a comprehensive undertaking. Cusanus's announcement of the reform measures was disseminated via the provincial or diocesan synods that met at locations along Cusanus's route in Salzburg, Bamberg, Magdeburg, Mainz, and Cologne. Orders were called together in general chapters, and special papal inspectors met with them. Noteworthy were the reforms in the Benedictine cloisters. These reforms were particularly well-documented in the Salzburg church province. Deserving special note were Cusanus's very positive efforts in the Bursfeld congregation, and likewise those with the Augustinian canons—for them Cusanus assigned Johannes Busch, the famous historian of the order, to be inspector—and, finally, the reforms of the mendicant orders.

Cusanus experienced bitter opposition from some of the mendicants. Later he even accused a member of the order of having extended a poisoned cross for him to kiss. Apparently it was doubtful whether the mendicant orders were as clearly subject to the authority of Cusanus's legation as the first legation bull of December 24, 1450, had in fact said. Regardless, Cusanus did not try to undertake any reforms of the mendicant orders until October 1451. At the request of the citizens of Sint Truiden he addressed the undisciplined life style of the Franciscans, and followed this by authorizing the parish to supervise the reform. Cusanus regarded the involvement of the laity as a very useful practice in general, and in Hildesheim and Cologne he gave the laity similar supervisory tasks. Of all the orders, the mendicants had the closest contact with the people, so when the order did something offensive, the effect on the religious life of the general populace was particularly serious. Cusanus's clear understanding of this phenomenon was coupled with his fundamental esteem for the layperson.

The mendicants used what Cusanus was doing to bring the gravest accusations against him. However, an indirect method by which Cusanus could get at the mendicants despite their exemption was to bring the bishops into play, since the mendicants were subject to the pastoral care of the bishops. This is the approach Cusanus used in Trier and at the provincial synods in Mainz and Cologne.

The Reform Plan Rejected

Experience tells us that it is usually resistance and conflict, and less often the joy of tranquility, that become known through reporting. Thus, it would be one-sided to conclude on the basis of the many legal appeals, the sharply formulated directives, and the significant number of proceedings meant to implement discipline and order by force that the reform journey was a great failure. For the internal life of the church in Germany it represented one of the most striking events of that period. It would be asking too much of this singular undertaking—one that went through the church like a powerful, yet brief storm—to conclude that the state of affairs in the year of Luther's Reformation was a result of its failure. In many places the high degree of discipline that persisted in orders for a long time, in part until secularization, can be traced back to the cardinal's measures. In some orders of **Canons Regular** his reform statutes remained in force until 1910. Finally, we might ask ourselves, what do we know about the spiritual comfort Cusanus brought, or about the renewal of hearts, even if this were for only one generation or less!

Nevertheless, Cusanus's reform undertaking cannot escape the judgment of history. From the start it was certainly an illusion to set the comprehensive goal of a general reform of the German church as provided for in the legation's papal bulls. Cusanus had to make this painful discovery as soon as he chaired the first provincial synod on his schedule. The synod was held in Salzburg at the beginning of February 1451. Cusanus presented a broad-sweeping list of regulations that, in its form, was no doubt meant to serve as a model for the other provinces of the German church. The document begins with stipulations about how to hold worship services in a dignified manner, deals with feast days and fasting, addresses the administration of the sacrament, and takes up the dignity of the priestly rank, from archbishop down to the least of the clergy. It treats with special emphasis the provincial and diocesan synods that are to be held periodically. It also deals with the bishops' **visitation** of clergy, stipulating above all more frequent visits, and speaks to the abuses (*circa mores et vitam*) to which the bishops should pay special attention during these visits. It goes into detail about the church's judicial system, and the casual attitude with which the church imposed penalties, as well as the shortcomings of the secular administration of justice that was particularly hard on the little person, and not least importantly, the document speaks to the issue of collectors of indulgence money.

The Salzburg clergy's response? "Go back to the drawing board." They meant, of course, "We prefer nothing at all." They argued that the regulations being promulgated were a matter for the German nation, and they in Salzburg could not accept them on their own. They said that a national council would have to be held, knowing this would obviously never come to pass. On the other hand, people knew that Cusanus was a staunch supporter of such a council. He had demonstrated this in Basel. Yet several months later when he brought forward the idea at the provincial council in Mainz people accused him of attempting surreptitiously to place the German church under Rome. They said the Curia should be so kind as to reform itself first before they would take orders from its legate.

For Cusanus there was no mistaking that the Salzburg plan had been wiped off the table, and we hear nothing about the plan being presented again at the subsequent provincial councils held during Cusanus's legation journey. Apparently Cusanus determined it was not workable, so his effort did not get beyond the already mentioned individual reform decrees that could be introduced only in scattered fashion here and there. It was the German church that resisted reform. Prior to any reform the Germans wanted the Curia to provide a corresponding guarantee of their rights.

To be sure, Cusanus's ecclesiastical policy, not least of all as a result of tensions in his theory of the church, resulted in a tension in church practice that apparently could not be resolved. On the one hand he considered the church, as he had already said in Basel, to be the community of believers united with Christ that becomes a reality as a community, synodically, and correspondingly makes a reality of sharing God's grace. On the other hand, an explicit aim of the reform journey was to reconnect the German church and nation with the pope, since they had distanced themselves from Rome during the conciliar movement. The reform decree that was documented most frequently on Cusanus's journey is the one that granted an indulgence of fifty days to any priest who inserted into the Sunday Mass specific prayers for his prelate, the pope, and the Catholic Church. However, again and again Cusanus had to take cognizance of the anti-Roman attitude that his mistrusting countrymen associated with their doubts about his honesty, even if they still professed, often emphatically, their adherence to the Roman Church.

Cusanus's Jewish Decree

We should not overlook another decree, one that was directed at the Jews. With an exactitude characteristic of Cusanus he gave orders that no later than stipulated deadlines all Jews had to wear identifying marks. The men had to display a saffron-yellow cloth ring on the breast of their jacket or coat; the women two blue stripes on their veil. By the same deadlines they were to cease all practices of usury with Christians. Only if Jews fulfilled these conditions would they be allowed to keep their homes. If they failed to observe the rules, an interdict would automatically be imposed on the parish in which they lived, and during the length of the interdict no priest would be allowed to celebrate Mass.

With this decree Cusanus was merely drawing on the corresponding Jewish decree from the Council of Basel in 1434. This decree had its own long history in which the regulations set by the fourth Lateran Council of 1215 were particularly influential. Thus, Cusanus stood within the conciliar tradition. The popes, on the other hand, were more tolerant, granting the Jews exceptions to the rules and letters of protection. Eugenius IV and Nicholas V are two who followed this practice. They said that the guilt the Jews had brought upon themselves certainly relegated them to permanent subjugation, yet Christian compassion (*pietas*) allowed them to live where they were, affording them "cohabitation" with Christians.

Since Christians who were in business were forbidden to charge interest, Jews continued to be very welcome as lenders. For this reason the people of Nuremberg, for example, and even the emperor, protested to the pope against Cusanus's Jewish Decree. The Nurembergers made the argument that the decree would produce wholly unintended consequences. That is, if the Jews could no longer make a living by lending money, then, like the Christians, they would have to take up trades in order to earn an income. This would be detrimental to all tradesmen and lead only to conflict. Consequently, it would be better for everyone if the Jews were lenders rather than workers. Within a short time Nicholas V did, in fact, rescind the legate's Jewish Decree, after already having postponed its effective date several times. It is difficult to pass proper judgment on Cusanus's obvious bias in favor of tradition. The historian must repeatedly deal with such difficulties. The circles of church reformers of the day were precisely the ones who displayed conspicuous hostility toward the Jews.

Difficulties in Deciding Disputes

Measured by Cusanus's success, the year 1451 marks the culmination of his career. Apart from his defeat in the Manderscheid dispute, he had advanced from victory to victory. Now, while the importance of his assignments was to keep increasing, good fortune would no longer be his faithful companion. When, from time to time, success eludes him we search for the deeper causes of his misfortune. Are the causes to be found in the issues themselves, or are they to be found in Cusanus's character, as one whose resiliency, tested to its limits, is diminishing? Or are they to be found in a disparity between the man and the mission, with the tasks simply exceeding the capacity of one individual?

In 1450 the pope had entrusted Cusanus not only with bringing inner peace to souls, but also with bestowing outward, political peace on the conflict-ridden country. On the day Cusanus was named legate, Nicholas V turned over to him the task of resolving the struggle between Cologne and Cleves. Efforts in the 1440s to effect unity in the church were strained by armed conflict in the empire. Pillaging and plundering were ruining the land. Not without good reason Cusanus had devoted extensive passages of *The Catholic Concordance* to peace and order in the empire.

In the northwest a dispute had broken out that was to last for years. It was inflamed by the ambitions of Dieter von Moers, archbishop of Cologne. The strife was primarily with the Dukes of Cleves, first as the Feud of Soest and then as the Münster Diocesan Feud. After Dieter had overextended himself with his expansionist policies and had aroused the opposition of his neighbors who felt their existence threatened, he found himself on the defensive in both feuds. Pope Eugenius IV, in order to compel the Duke of Cleves to come over to his side, even supported the duke's efforts to establish his own bishopric of Xanten. The pope thereby lent support to the problematic territorial church structure that was to become such a decisive factor in church history in the following centuries. The Curia immediately abandoned this policy when Dieter humbly gave in.

Beginning in 1446 Cusanus and Carvajal, the papal legates, took up the Cologne-Cleves dispute. Through this task they found out how difficult peace talks—indeed, negotiations of any kind—were to be in the entangled networks of secular and spiritual authority. Cusanus experienced this more deeply than Carvajal since the greater burden in the mediation process fell to him. Cusanus was the chief author of the decision that Carvajal pronounced in Maastricht on April 27, 1449. With it the Feud of Soest came to an end, and Cusanus and the Count of the Mark were appointed protectors of the peace.

However, in 1450 fighting broke out anew when Dieter, upon

the death of his brother, the bishop of Münster, set about to name another brother as successor. In 1451 and 1452 Cusanus struggled in vain to settle the new conflict. We observe how he lost his patience too quickly during the negotiations and forfeited his chance for success. He had a good personal relationship with both sides that led him to be sympathetic to both. However, precisely this considerate behavior caused his contrasting, sudden outbreaks of nervous harshness to produce a particularly unfavorable effect. To a great extent this harshness was influenced by Cusanus's strong desire that, no matter what, peace should be restored under his leadership. Since he would be leaving Germany in the spring of 1452, he was under the constraint of time. Perhaps this lack of time pressured him into his clumsily rash actions.

Not only in the Münster affair but in the numerous decisions Cusanus had to make in the controversies brought before him he demonstrated a fundamental bias. Despite his high regard for the laity, whenever ecclesiastical institutions or individuals stood in opposition to secular ones, Cusanus gave priority—unless everything spoke against it—to safeguarding the rights of the church. For example, the citizens of the imperial city of Weißenburg had plundered the Benedictine cloister of Wülzburg, located outside their city gates. They considered the cloister to be a supply station for Margrave Albert Achilles, with whom they had a feud. Cusanus imposed the church's severest penalties on the citizens. It is unclear to what extent the pope caused Cusanus to reverse his decision, but he eventually withdrew the penalties. Similarly, in Lüneburg's conflict with the provost of Lüne Cusanus sided with the provost and against the city.

It is difficult to draw general conclusions from Cusanus's handling of this and other controversies. One needs to examine them case by case—if the state of the official records even makes this possible—to see whether each one might not be a matter of this or that local law. On the other hand, Cusanus was not familiar with local circumstances, and his level of knowledge depended entirely on the reports that reached him. Thus, as critical as people here and there were of him, especially when he decided against them, he continued to enjoy lively competition from those trying to curry his favor.

Peace and the Rising Nation States

In vain Cusanus kept wishing he could dedicate himself to a task he considered significant. On December 29, 1450, the pope commissioned him to work toward the reunification of the Bohemians with the church. A variety of difficulties stood in the way of his plans. His involvement with affairs in Brixen was a great hindrance, although it probably saved him from an additional failure in Bohemia. Over the course of time his approach to the Bohemian question became increasingly inconsistent. Some accused Cusanus of being sympathetic to the heretics. In 1462 he himself cast a vote to revoke the *Compactata,* by which the Council of Basel, with his involvement, had attempted to conclude a settlement.

Cusanus had a similar experience in the West. On August 13, 1451, the pope designated him, in expanding the legation's authority to England, to be peace negotiator between England and France in their Hundred Years War. He was supposed to cross over to the British Isles, while the French Cardinal Guillaume d'Estouteville would meet with the French king. Since the initiative for negotiations had come from Duke Philip the Good of Burgundy, the pope instructed his German legate to put himself in contact with the duke. One month later the pope sent twenty additional bulls to Cusanus with expanded authority for absolutions, dispensations and promotions. The legate was to arrive in England with his hands full of good things. The favors of the Jubilee Year would be evidence of the overflowing blessings of peace.

As we have already heard, in January Cusanus traveled back to Brussels from Cologne for a surprise visit with Philip. Then, however, he did not head to England. We do not know exactly why, but one hint is that he had just received the news that the advisors of King Henry VI had unceremoniously turned away the papal nuncio Marino Orsini, who had been sent in advance of Cusanus.

In 1455 Pope Calixtus III once again gave the cardinal the assignment to negotiate peace. Cusanus's trip, with the aim of arousing England in view of the Turkish threat against the western world, was of pressing importance. Cusanus informed King Henry VI of his decision to make the journey, and he received 1000 ducats in advance from the pope. Everything was ready when the king replied to Cusanus that he ought to stay home. According to the king, peace negotiations and crusades were utopian as long as the King of France was robbing him of cities and territories, and furthermore, the King of Scotland had, without warning, broken the peace and invaded England. Since, according to Henry VI, the French king had broken every treaty up to now, the hope of easing tensions was illusory.

In connection with the English legation we hear a new theme: unity of the western world. Although we do not encounter the theme again for some time, it appears toward the end of Cusanus's life with all the more strength. While unity of the church had been regained in 1448—discounting the Bohemians and the strengthening of Gallicanism through the proclamation of the **Pragmatic Sanction of Bourges** in 1438—the rivalry among the increasingly powerful nation states signified an ever-present danger. Moreover, the growing consolidation within each separate state was also leading to problems for the church like those that had arisen in Bourges.

According to Leopold Ranke, modern history as history of the European system of states begins in 1494 with the invasion of

Naples by Charles VIII. This system of states is characterized by an interplay of forces that presupposes the pluralism of individual states. Unity in this system consists solely of interrelationships, relationships that can be purely those of war. But this is not the relationship of participants as Cusanus understood it. His unity has in its connections among the participants an everlasting, universal element. The system of powers did not correspond to the image he had in mind as he worked for unity in the western world.

The Brixen Controversy Begins

On March 23, 1450, Nicholas V appointed the cardinal to be bishop of Brixen, bestowing the office on him on April 26. The position had become free on February 28, and on March 14 three representatives of the chapter chose their fellow canon, Leonard Wismayer, to be successor. Wismayer was a priest from Tyrol, advisor and chancellor of Duke Sigismund of Austria and count of Tyrol. For Cusanus this initiated a destructive tragedy that we can sketch with only a few strokes rather than presenting the large picture that the historian would like to paint in greater detail. History, in its multitude of many-layered complexities, confronted Cusanus once again.

Election versus appointment—so it started. This was nothing unusual in the history of the ecclesiastical office system: a three-way contention among free elections, the independent rights of the chapter, and the claims of the chief office of the church. For years Nicholas himself had defended Ulrich von Manderscheid, the "elected," against Raban, the "appointed." Now he, too, was the "appointed" one. Just as once the pope had annulled the election of Ulrich, so now he annulled the election in Brixen. In his view it had not been free, but had been carried out under pressure from the duke. In the case of Ulrich the pressure had come from the nobility of Trier. This fact, of course, reveals the first difference in the two cases. Brixen was, like Trier, a principality, but in

Trier it was the principality itself that wanted to elect the ruler, while in Brixen it was an outside prince.

Sigismund naturally proceeded under protection of the law. As guardian of the church of Brixen he was responsible for its peace and protection. In fact, his father, Duke Frederick IV, had already gone about incorporating Brixen into his territory. Its relationship to Tyrol would be similar to that of the cathedral chapters of Chur and Trent. In Eichstätt the Wittelsbachs had made a similar effort and with the cathedral chapters under their authority, finally drew in the Brandenburgers and Wettiners.

In Trier, as in Brixen, the laity had threatened to infringe on the clergy's authority. For Nicholas, the fundamental difference was that in Brixen the infringement was of necessity at the heart of the conflict, whereas in Trier it became a problem only through unreasonable rejection of the laity's demands. Thus, the two cases were fundamentally different. In Trier the canon would have been supported by the subjects. In Brixen he would be set above the subjects and, as the favored private chaplain of the duke, would be answering to a secular ruler. If a further sharpening of the contrast is allowed, in Trier the estate-related, corporative principle was to be put into practice, whereas in Brixen it was the princely, absolutist principle.

One might, of course, reproach Cusanus, the bishop, for pursuing antiquated policies in defending his interests as head of a principality. After all, sooner or later the church would have to bid farewell to the secular grandeur that the imperial Ottonian-Salian ecclesiastical policy had once officially ratified and even bestowed on the church. However, this would be unfair to him, for who could have anticipated in 1450 that the Principle Decree of the Imperial Deputation of 1803 would give Brixen and Trent to Austria? As a matter of fact, they had already been excluded in Chur in 1526 when the three allies secularized the bishopric.

In order to understand Cusanus, let us measure him by the only possible standard, namely the historical reality of his time. This reality presented itself to him in the massive amount of pressure that Sigismund exerted on the church in Brixen. A papal bull of October 31, 1450, which naturally was influenced by Nicholas, goes beyond the lack of freedom in the election of March 14 to the fundamental assertion: "We have acted on proper grounds, since we know from the past and present that the power of the duke would make any free election impossible." This means that Nicholas knew from the beginning what awaited him in Brixen, and it was not a minor disagreement. What was at stake was the freedom of the Brixen church from the grasp of the prince.

No doubt Cusanus talked over the situation candidly with his papal friend. We presume he would not have to assume the bishopric if he had resisted. However, if he were to take the office, then he would do it with the determination to accept the office as a challenge—one that was too burdensome, as was to become clear, one that he perhaps underestimated, but not one that was a necessary evil. If it had been a question of just any bishopric he would have let Brixen go when everything turned against him, when, driven out and in flight, he never saw his church again, and when people suggested that he ought to give it up in exchange for the prospect of material gain.

At the end of the 1440s Nicholas negotiated with the archbishop of Trier to change the legal status of the parish church of St. Wendel, for which Nicholas was the priest. The right to appoint the parish's priest belonged to the archbishop, though according to the church's geographical divisions St. Wendel was situated in the Metz diocese. One alternative was to elevate St. Wendel, as a suffragan bishopric of Trier, to be a cathedral church, thus freeing it from the connection to Metz. Should the serving priest, Cusanus, become the first bishop? We would do well to regard Cusanus's deep sense of duty as a major influence on his actions. This view helps us understand that he took on the responsibilities in Brixen thanks to an inborn energetic spirit, without which, in the final analysis, his historical persona would be difficult to understand.

The Conflict Unfolds

The first flare-up of the Brixen dispute was quickly extinguished. Ecclesiastical penalties threatened by the pope were postponed several times. On his trip to Germany in the winter of 1451 Nicholas avoided his diocese. In Wiener Neustadt he made sure of the emperor's help. In Salzburg an agreement was reached on March 15 with Wismayer, who withdrew, while Cusanus promised Duke Sigismund friendship and loyalty. Was the duke assuming that Cardinal Cusanus would not reside in Brixen but, entrusted with other ecclesiastical duties, would regard his bishop's church as only a sinecure?

Initially Nicholas showed himself to be completely open to compromise in matters that came up. For example, at the beginning of January 1452, while still in Cologne, he instructed his vicar-general in Brixen to comply with the duke's choice regarding appointment of a priest for Zams. Nicholas added that, as bishop, it was actually his right to confer the office, and the vicar-general was to make this point clear with the duke. In order to demonstrate fully his good will Nicholas directed his vicar-general to use the assistance of Leonard Wismayer to install the candidate who had been presented by the duke.

Yet how long could Cusanus justify these individual acts within the context of his fundamental position? In April 1452, determined to lift the bishopric and church out of the spiritual and material depths to which they had sunk under his predecessors, Cusanus took over the administrative affairs. He was greeted by a considerable debt. On May 12, 1453, he secured from the pope the regulation: "The bishops of Brixen will use all the table taxes from the first year for eliminating debts and paying off mortgaged castles and lands of their church. They can become neither chancellors nor personal chaplains of secular princes, since they must govern their church personally." On December 7, 1452, the emperor gave Cusanus ownership of all saltworks and mines in the bishopric. In the following month Cusanus demanded from the lords of Freundsberg the return of Steinach and Matrei, which had been mortgaged to them, and he placed under his protection from a takeover by the Sonnenburg convent those in Enneberg who were loyal to the bishop.

These actions stirred up new problems, first of all in his personal relationship to Duke Sigismund. The duke was accustomed to having the bishop of Brixen do what he wished. The natural result was that the bishop was treated patronizingly like an obedient servant. Nicholas, the cardinal of St. Peter in Chains, who, after taking up the episcopal office, was still apostolic legate for a long time, was not about to let himself be classified as a vassal. Earlier we gained insight into the importance for Cusanus, as a son of the middle class, of the issue of rank. Thus, we can appreciate why, in dealing with the Austrian duke, he put stronger emphasis on his ecclesiastical office than was strategically wise.

The conflict with the duke about rank and class repeated itself in the relationship of our cardinal from the house of Krebs with the Tyrolean nobility. Although Sigismund was nicknamed the "Duke of Ducats," he was constantly short of money. The duke's financial mismanagement had led to greater authority of the provincial diets in Tyrol as well as in other locations in Germany, primarily due to their intervention into the duke's financial affairs. Through their increased power, the Tyrolean nobles felt that their honor and rank had also been enhanced. In Sonnenburg the **Abbess** Verena von Stuben presided over a circle of cloistered noblewomen who were well provided for by their families. It was not to be expected that they, no more than their fathers and brothers from the Inn to the Eisack and Drava, would let someone who had not sprung from their class and who, moreover, was an outsider, tell them anything.

People have criticized Cusanus for being unable, as a Rhinelander, to adapt to the Tyrolean mentality, but when we see the affection that ordinary people in the diocese repeatedly showed him we have to believe that the criticism is not of great significance. Even so, after the clash in Brixen had already broken out for other reasons, his inability to understand the character of the local people as well as his inability to get along with conditions in the alpine world did add to the tension.

Flight

The fact that the bishop and duke, despite passing conflicts, remained in a reasonable relationship until the beginning of 1457 testifies to the self-control and patience on both sides. In 1454, after Nicholas had paid off the debts of his predecessor, and after he had called in the episcopal loans under threat of penalties from the church, with the result that the income from their rewritten versions was brought under better control, he began to buy back the numerous properties that had been used as security for loans. On April 18, 1454, after taking back Steinach and Matrei, he recalled the ecclesiastical offices of St. Petersberg and Straßberg from Freundsberg. The strategically important location of Steinach and Matrei on the Brenner Pass before the gates of Innsbruck filled Sigismund with particular concern. On September 16, 1455, Nicholas redeemed the court of Velturn that the duke had passed on to Asam von Kastlan as collateral. Finally, on March 18, 1456, the bishop purchased the office of Taufers above Bruneck, simultaneously granting the duke a handsome amount of credit. The purchase price surpassed the value of the object to a considerable degree. Sigismund tolerated the consolidation of the Brixen church because the bishop was helping him out in his financial need.

During this whole time, Duke Sigismund had to smooth things out with the nobility since it lost some of its income through Cusanus's resolute policy. However, the nobility was upset primarily by what the bishop did with the Sonnenburg cloister and with other institutions and cloisters of the bishopric. In the case of Sonnenburg he came into conflict mainly in his role as ruler of the territory, while in other places he pursued exclusively religious aims, concerning himself only with the necessity for reform. He not only regarded his attention to the discipline of the clergy and orders in his diocese to be a continuation of his legation work, but he also wanted to demonstrate how a model bishopric should look.

However, the initially peaceful relationship Nicholas had with Duke Sigismund was in part a result of the duke's quiet assent to a number of strict measures that Nicholas took the liberty of imposing on the nobility. Often, upon a complaint by Nicholas, Sigismund would admonish his subjects to observe the rights of the Brixen church. Perhaps this approach would have enabled Nicholas and the duke to continue to get along if the nobility's opposition had not eventually forced the duke to give up this strategy. Cusanus's reform efforts exposed an intransigence that worked in favor of the nobility. In addition, the bishop made a very unfortunate decision.

Leonard Wismayer, whom the pope had disallowed from being bishop of Brixen, was elected bishop of neighboring Chur. When he made the move to Chur in 1456, the majority of the cathedral chapter in Brixen, where Wismayer had been a member, transferred Wismayer's prebend, on Cusanus's recommendation, to Cusanus's nephew, Simon von Wehlen. Wismayer wanted to keep control of his Brixen prebend for the time being, and four Brixen

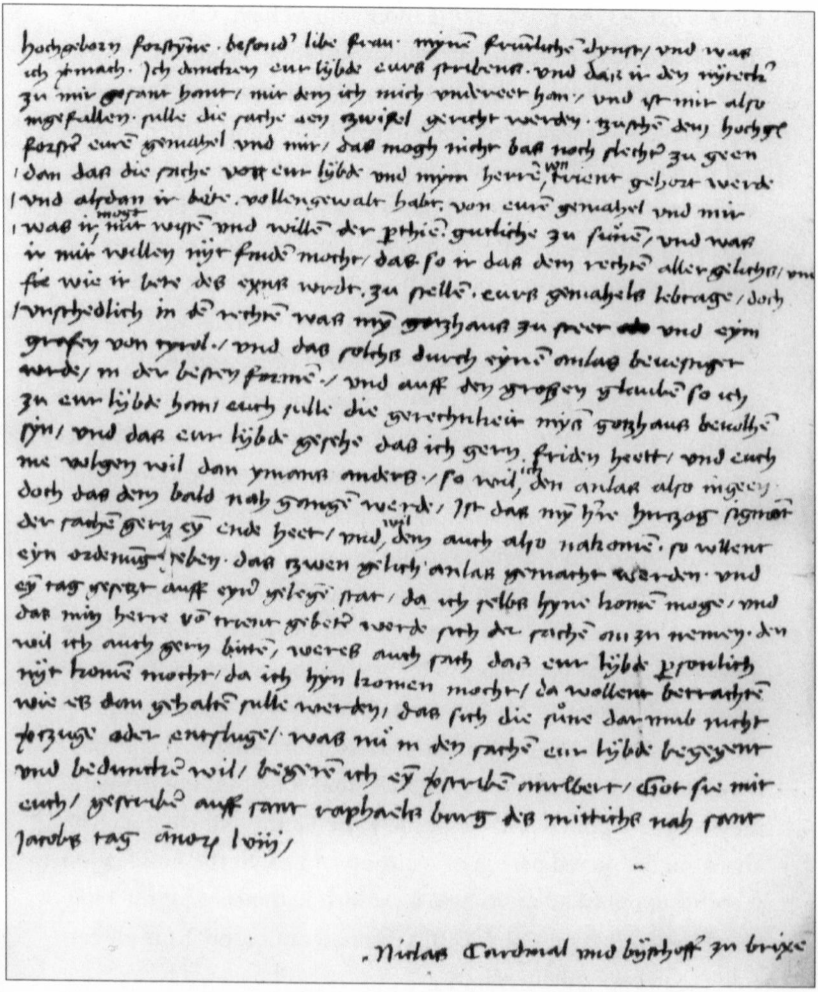
hochgeborn furstynne . besunder libe frau . mynen fruntlichen dynst / vnd was
ich vermach . Ich dancken eur lybde eurs schribens . vnd das ir den nyrecht
zu mir gesant hant / mit dem ich mich vnderreet han / vnd ist mir also
ingefallen . sulle die sache aen zwifel gericht werden . zuschen dem hochge
born eurem gemahel vnd mir / das mogh nicht bas noch slechter zu geen
/ dan das die sache vor eur lybde vnd mynem herren von trient gehort werde
/ vnd alsdan ir beide vollengewalt haben von eurem gemahel vnd mir
/ was ir mogt nach wysen vnd willen der partie gutlichen zu sunen / vnd was
ir mit willen nyt finden mocht / das so ir das dem rechten aller gelichest / vm
sie wie ir bede des eyns werdt . zu stellen . eurs gemahels lebtage / doch
/ vnschedlich in den rechten was myn gotzhaus zu steet vnd eym
grafen von tyrol . / vnd das solchs durch eynen anlas bevestiget
werde / in der besten forme . / vnd auff den grossen glauben so ich
zu eur lybde han / euch sulle die gerechtikeit myns gotzhaus bevolhen
syn / vnd das eur lybde gesehe das ich gern frieden hett / vnd euch
me volgen wil dan ymants anders . / so wil ich den anlas also ingeen
doch das dem bald nah gangen werde / Ist das myn herre herzog sigmunt
der sachen gern ein ende heet / vnd wil dem auch also nahkomen . so wollent
eyn ordenunge geben . das zwen gelich anlas gemacht werden . vnd
eyn tag gesetzt auff eyn gelegen stat / da ich selbs hyn komen moge / vnd
das myn herre von trient gebeten werde sich der sachen an zu nemen . dan
wil ich auch gern bitten / weres auch sach das eur lybde personlich
nyt komen mocht / da ich hyn komen mocht / da wollent betrachten
wie es dan gehalten sulle werden / das sich die sune darumb nicht
verzuge ader entsluge / was nu in den sachen eur lybde begegent
vnd bedunchen wil / begere ich eyn schriben antwort / Got sie mit
euch / geschriben auff sant raphaels burg des mitwochs nah sant
Jacobs tag anno lviij /

. Niclas Cardinal vnd bysshoff zu brixe

FIGURE 7. Cusanus writes from the fortress of Saint Raphael at Buchenstein, July 26, 1458, to Duchess Eleanore, wife of Sigismund, requesting that she negotiate with the Bishop of Trent. "I would like to have peace," he writes, yet "without detriment to the rights that belong to my house of God and to a Count of Tyrol."

canons denied the transfer to Simon von Wehlen. Cardinal Cusanus immediately excommunicated them. They responded with an
appeal. At the end of a Sunday Mass a fight almost broke out when
they forced their way into the church in order to read their appeal,
and confronted Nicholas as he was leaving the chancel. The "case"
of Simon von Wehlen offered the nobility a welcome opportunity
to turn opinion against the bishop once and for all. The illustrious
circle of the Brixen chapter, which up to now had been a close-knit
group, was supposed to put up with the bishop's relative.

During the year things gradually deteriorated until Sigismund,
pressured by the grievances over Brixen and Sonnenburg, finally
decided to break with the bishop. Apparently he had studied his
opponent carefully over the last few years in order to confirm a
very personal weakness in Cusanus, namely anxiety, fear for his
life. Building on this, Sigismund intimidated Cusanus with threats
during the bishop's stay in Innsbruck. As Cusanus was returning
to Brixen the duke feigned an attack with the intent of murdering
him. This caused Nicholas, no longer feeling secure in Brixen, to
retreat in July 1457 to his fortress at Buchenstein, far back among
the steep cliffs on the edge of his diocese. Here he stayed until September 1458. With all the ostentation one might expect, he naturally let the whole world—especially the Curia—know about the
attack on the sacred person of a bishop and about the humiliation
that this unpunished menace to a cardinal had meant for the Holy
See. However, Pope Calixtus III refrained noticeably from threatening to impose an interdict.

On August 19, 1458, Aeneas Sylvius, humanist and friend of
Cusanus, ascended the papal throne as Pius II. He had already appealed to Nicholas in 1456 and 1457 not to squander his energy "in
the snow and dark valleys," but to come to Rome and share his
counsel with the entire church. In September 1458 Cusanus left his
fortress and arrived in Rome on September 30.

Gregor Heimburg Enters the Fray

Mediation between Sigismund and Cusanus by Pius II did not seem to be out of the question since the pope had been closely acquainted with the young duke at the imperial court. Pius advised the cardinal not to be unbending, since the pope wanted to win over the duke for his great undertaking, the crusade of the West against the Turks. Yet it was at this very moment that an unfortunate circumstance destroyed all hope for a peaceful resolution.

In May 1458 Gregor Heimburg entered into the service of Duke Sigismund. Heimburg combined his old personal hatred of Nicholas with a fundamental opposition to the papacy, carrying away from the Council of Basel the concept of a German church free of Rome. In preceding years Nicholas and Heimburg had fallen into vehement disputes. The crafty, unwavering anticurialist utilized the intervention of the pope in Brixen like a new grievance (*gravamina*) of the German nation. He had connections with the Bohemians and papal opposition wherever it was forming in the empire. In 1461 he even worked toward bringing together in a new conciliar coalition Diether von Isenburg, Archbishop of Mainz, who opposed the policies of the pope, the Brixen dispute about the Bohemian opposition, and the tendencies toward a national church in France.

The preventative countermeasures of Pope Pius II worked decidedly against Heimburg. These were, among others, his bull *Execrabilis,* of January 18, 1460, that prohibited appeals to a council. Yet Heimburg was hindered most by the impossibility, after the experience of Basel, of uniting once again the anticurial forces to form a council without the pope. Nevertheless, the larger context into which the conflict over Brixen was thereby placed attests to its significance in the history of the German church.

Could Nicholas respond to such complications? Was he not

aware of other consequences that continuation of the conflict would precipitate? The struggle would be carried out essentially by judicial means, that is, with the help of excommunication and interdict that his papal friend had to pronounce not only on his opponents but also on the believers in Brixen who were innocent of the whole affair. The results would be inexorable: setbacks in the moral renewal for which he had been struggling for five years; the lack of spiritual care for those excluded from the sacraments; the end of worship services. Did the cause outweigh these sacrifices?

Cusanus believed the purity of the church could not be assured without its freedom, and freedom seemed impossible without material independence. This is the basis on which he defended his secular claims. He considered it his indisputable duty to prevent any diminishment of the property of the Brixen church entrusted to him as bishop, as well as to guard its rights, and where they had been lost, to win them back. To what extent his personal, stubborn intransigence—insisting on his rights—was an additional factor, to what extent his deeply human engagement that simply could not accept defeat played a role, and to what extent his injured pride brought out his real obstinacy—all this defies precise determination. Yet these factors clearly resonate between the lines in Cusanus's letters that provide information about the Brixen conflict. An additional factor that Cusanus himself sensed was the hardly bearable thought that, in the final analysis, a resolution could be achieved only if he were to step down. Absent is a vision that could have served as the basis for negotiations.

Cusanus Surrenders to Sigismund

On November 10, 1459, Duke Sigismund appeared at the Congress of Mantua that Pope Pius had called in preparation for the crusade against the Turks. There the duke expressed a cooperative attitude in regard to the question of Brixen. However, could

Bishop Cusanus think seriously that Sigismund would let him rule in Brixen as he had? What chances did Nicholas see for himself when, at the beginning of the next year, he decided to return for a short time?

Sigismund waited for his opponent to make just one mistake so that he could strike once and for all. Again the bishop saw armed men everywhere, but nothing happened to him yet. Even so, he moved from Brixen to Bruneck, and shortly thereafter still further to the fortress of Buchenstein, since he did not consider even Bruneck to be safe. He regarded the threat of force to be a reality, and he parried with the counterthreat of giving back all the landholdings of the Brixen church to the emperor. Sigismund viewed this as grounds for war and gathered his army. Meanwhile Nicholas had returned to Bruneck, so the duke's soldiers surrounded the town. The town surrendered; the shelling of the fortress began.

Documents that declared the Duke's terms of victory were presented to the cardinal for him to affix his seal. So it was that Cusanus, this great personage, the prince of the church, found himself in the hour of his deepest humiliation, abandoned by his troops that Captain Prack held back in Buchenstein! Cusanus submitted to the victor's power and put his seal on everything Sigismund laid before him. This included the return of Taufers; the forgiveness of a debt of 3,000 gulden that Sigismund had assumed under Cusanus as well as 10,000 gulden in ransom money; and the transfer of all episcopal fortresses to the chapter, which had to keep them permanently open to the duke and assign them commanders of whom he approved. Furthermore, Cusanus gave up the right to reclaim any estates that the duke had taken over from his father, and he agreed to lift as quickly as possible the interdict he had imposed a few weeks earlier, and to obtain from the pope the absolution of the duke for his malicious action at Bruneck.

Scarcely freed, Cusanus did precisely what the duke could have expected. He declared all the agreements invalid because, he argued, he had signed them under duress. He would be unable to intercede with the pope on Sigismund's behalf unless the duke returned all the property he had taken from the bishopric. The speed with which Cusanus made this announcement, already on a stopover in Ampezzano only five days after the Agreements of Bruneck, indicates the turbulence of those days. It is said that in Buchenstein a furious Cusanus ordered that his Captain Prack be hanged from the bars of a window since Prack had not protected him in Bruneck. Two months later Cusanus wrote to the bishop of Eichstätt, "I was hoping to be able to end my last day in a glorious death for the cause of justice. I was not worthy of it."

This statement testifies to Cusanus's uncommon openness. In Christian humility he confessed his failure. Naturally, a person who looks at this objectively must ask seriously whether it actually would have been necessary for Cusanus to put his life at risk, whether this risk would have been worth it, and whether the risk could have been justified morally and theologically in the first place. Let us judge Nicholas of Cusa according to his own view of the events. His interpretation hides nothing, defends nothing, testifies to the courage of his spirit and conscience, and reveals the grace that shows its strength in the weak. In the same letter to the bishop of Eichstätt he posed the question of whether the secular power of the church was not indeed problematic. One could accuse Cusanus of putting his life at stake for merely earthly goods. Yet, if these goods were to secure the freedom of the church and the freedom for reform, at Bruneck he would have been giving them up indirectly. If he had come to the conclusion that secular power was not necessary, surrender at Bruneck would have meant surrender of his Brixen policies.

In Cusanus's case all of this has nothing to do with a deficiency in the courage of his faith, despite what Karl Jaspers presumed.

Cusanus's struggle to find the right way and his humble recognition of the imperfection of all earthly activity—something he experienced not least of all within himself—gave him an understanding of the meaning of death that he expressed in one of his last writings, "Do not think you are praying if you do not struggle to the point of death and arise from prayer soaked in sweat, spattered with your blood, and at least *in a spiritual way* burned by hot tears."

Resolution

News of the events in Bruneck reached the Curia as quick as the wind. The situation could not have been more untimely for Pope Pius and his crusade. Now he had to defend papal authority that had been attacked in the person of the cardinal. Apparently Nicholas, in accordance with the agreements at Bruneck, interceded on behalf of Sigismund so that the pope temporarily postponed the church's punishments due Sigismund. Despite all attempts at a settlement, Sigismund's recalcitrance, hardened by Gregor Heimburg, led in August 1460 to the imposition of the most severe censures.

We have room here for only a few words about the events of the next four years. The ban and interdict on the duke were followed by the agitation of his neighbors against him. The members of the Swiss Confederation took advantage of the opportunity to take over the Austrian border territories in Switzerland in order to get them permanently under their control. A settlement of the conflict became more and more urgent because of the spiritual needs of the faithful in the Brixen diocese. The emperor and doge intervened, and finally in 1464 negotiations at the royal court paved the way for a settlement.

On June 2, 1464, an agreement was reached whereby Nicholas was to remain bishop, although a representative was to take his place to carry out the duties of the office. The granting of benefices would remain in Nicholas's hands, and the income from the table tax was also to continue to be his. On June 12 the emperor ordered the return of Taufers and all the bishop's estates that had been seized after the attack. The bishop was to turn over to the duke all tenured landholdings. Sigismund gave the emperor full authority to seek absolution for him from the pope. On August 25 the seal was affixed to the documents and on September 2 Frederick III solicited from the papal legates absolution for Sigismund.

As the agreement demonstrates, the main issue when all is said and done was the personages and their prestige. Let us give the bishop the benefit of the doubt when he insisted on his rights because of the dignity of his office, because of the Roman Church, and even for the glory of God. However, Nicholas, if anyone, had to be troubled by the thought that by insisting on his rights he was destroying the more important thing, the seeds of spiritual renewal that he had sown in his diocese. For one can say without reservation that while he pressed very hard to obtain the office of bishop, certainly no other German bishop in his century carried out the office with as much pastoral devotion as he.

Detailed Regulations for Church Reform

Reform of the diocese was to proceed systematically from the top down. Until the time Nicholas took office as bishop of Brixen only three diocesan synods had been held in Brixen in the fifteenth century, and even these were only repetitions of the preceding Salzburg provincial synods. In 1453 Nicholas ordered that synods be held annually in accordance with the directives of the Council of Basel. Using all necessary means he achieved this until the year 1457, except in 1456. In view of the difficult travel conditions in mountainous Tyrol, the synods placed a burdensome demand on the clergy, and, alas, the first synod made this clear, since it was held in February 1453—this meant in ice and snow.

Nicholas himself did not shrink from any path in his bishopric. This shepherd was known by his sheep in even the most remote mountainside pastures and isolated valleys. He dedicated churches and chapels, granted indulgences, went on inspection visits, and made arrangements for everyday affairs of church life. In all of this he was complying with the Basel synodical decree of 1433 that, as it affected him, he had already included in the statutes he laid before the Salzburg Provincial Council.

He set the stage for his visitation of the entire diocese in the spring of 1455 by drawing up regulations for the inspection. For this purpose he prepared a long questionnaire, and while it is true that he used a text by Jean Gerson as a starting point, he went far beyond Gerson. Gerson had desired that laity participate in visitations, but Nicholas emphasizes this even more. He has the laity taking an oath like clerics. Furthermore, Nicholas draws special attention to the proper supervision of church property, whereas Gerson says nothing about this. Even in small details the significance of material things did not escape Nicholas's eye. In planning for this pastoral activity Nicholas was influenced by similar efforts in Tegernsee. He was also in touch with his friend, the bishop, in Eichstätt.

Here are only a few of the numerous queries in Nicholas's long list of questions: Do foreign clerics have identity papers? Are any members of the order carrying out pastoral duties without the bishop's approval? Is the **breviary** used regularly according to the standards of the diocesan directorate? Are the eucharistic elements and the baptismal water stored properly? Do the clergy behave in a devout manner at Mass? In cases of illness or old age are they still able to celebrate properly? Are they **tonsured**, and do they wear decent vestments? Is there any prophesying, fortune-telling or practice of magic? Do the clergy have concubines? To whom do they make confession?

Nicholas devoted himself to numerous questions about pasto-

ral care. He forbade pilgrimages that were not granted approval
by church authorities. He reorganized the calendar of liturgical
festivals, doing away with a great number of special days. At the
Mainz Provincial Council at the beginning of December 1451 he
had already given out a generally binding calendar of feast days for
the German Church provinces of Mainz, Magdeburg, Cologne,
and Bremen, and he had already done this for Salzburg as well.
An exhortation to keep the feast days and Sundays holy accompanied the calendar. He had little interest in works righteousness.
He called upon the people not to set their hopes on things they
thought they could claim from God or even from his saints as a
result of their rigorous pilgrimages, but to leave in the hands of
divine providence the granting of favors for which they prayed.
What lay at the bishop's heart was, above all, the practice of confession and repentance. The ignorance he encountered about these
very practices caused him to make special arrangements for sermons about them for parish members who were unable to participate regularly in the Mass.

Annual gatherings of the clergy on the local level were meant
to support the practical implementation of what had been worked
out at the diocesan synods. Nicholas divided the diocese into three
regional chapters, over each of which a deputy of the bishop presided. In the periods between the chapter meetings the deputies
were to visit the parishes in their respective regions on a regular
basis and then report at the next diocesan synod.

Cusanus took a personal interest in the visitations down to
minor details. One time, for example, in the village of Albeins he
decided who was to have the key to the church's poor box as well
as to the storage place for the host and consecrated oil. He gave
orders that graves should be dug at least seven feet deep, and sex-
tons had to have a measuring stick on hand in order to verify the
depth. Seen from the distance of centuries, some of Nicholas's in-

structions might bring a smile, but viewed from the proximity of his day they reveal a pastoral care whose earnestness made him privy to the smallest needs of his people. With these and innumerable other regulations he tried to address the spiritual need he saw everywhere in daily life. We might admire the lofty flights of Cusanus's speculation, his thoughts about the universal nature of the church and about its fundamental structure, but if the honor of human greatness—taking into account all his failures—can be conferred on Cusanus, it can be done in recognition of this devotion to everyday life. In his grasp of both the great and the small lies proof of the truly humane universality of his character.

Concern for Matters Great and Small

Precisely in small matters Cusanus proceeded with careful deliberation. For example, in 1455 several master weavers in the bishopric came to Cusanus to complain about the competition from itinerant journeymen from Friaul. The competition from these weavers was detrimental to the bishopric, too, since the outside weavers paid no taxes. Therefore Cusanus forbade all his subjects to give work to traveling weavers, but he ordered the local weavers to charge only appropriate sums, meaning that they were not to practice price-gouging, in which they would be exploiting the monopoly of which they had been assured. A few years earlier Sigismund, too, had, for the protection of the master tailors in Innsbruck, forbidden outside journeymen from practicing their craft in the city because they neither paid taxes nor shared in defraying other public costs. However, he failed to include the simultaneous protection of the rest of the population, as Cusanus had. Was not Nicholas the more just sovereign who in each instance looked out for the well-being of all his subjects?

Cusanus's care was coupled again and again with great strictness. We do not know whether the stern manner in which he treated the clerics brought him at least short-term success. In any case, we learn that in 1460 the farmers of Buchenstein, when they found out about the attack in Bruneck, seized their weapons in order to free their pastor. It is also uncertain whether the reformer was always understood when he intervened in the religious practices of pilgrimages and **sacramentals** that were shaped by folk custom. This realm of religious life was apt to be more sacrosanct for simple believers than the dogma they were unable to comprehend with their intellect. For the present, our verdict must be based on the endeavors of the bishop, and must consider them to have been proper, clear-sighted, and sometimes perhaps too stern, while it leaves the assessment of success to a higher being.

Armed Conflict

In contrast to the little information we have about the effect of Nicholas's reforms on simple believers, we are much better informed about the conflicts that his cloister reforms stirred up. These led straight to the final catastrophe. On May 2, 1452, he posted the reform decrees pronounced at the Salzburg Provincial Synod stipulating reform of the orders and cloistering of the nuns in the convents in Brixen. Yet, after a year had passed, six monasteries and convents—Stams, Wilten, Georgenberg, Neustift, Sonnenburg, and the **Poor Clares** of Brixen—had not complied with anything. On May 12, 1453, the pope gave Nicholas special full powers of authority over these places. First of all Nicholas dealt with the Poor Clares. Not until he had removed the nuns who came from the nobility, brought seven Poor Clares from Nuremberg to the nunnery, and replaced the local abbess with one from outside, did he break the resistance. He dealt similarly with Wilten, to which he brought a prior from Magdeburg. Maria von Wolkenstein, a Poor Clare from Brixen, wrote during these days to her brother, Frederick von Wolkenstein: "The bishop also declared that he is not impressed with the Wolkensteiners or any other sovereigns." In their pride the nuns from the aristocratic class did not put up with this disdain of their background.

In the Benedictine convent of Sonnenburg at Bruneck opposition grew into boundless hatred of the unflappable reformer who was so convinced of the great importance of his task. Moreover, from the very beginning the religious issues in Sonnenburg were encumbered with secular controversies. The nuns were mired in conflict with people from Enneberg who were in the convent's territory. Since the convent had certain rights in Enneberg the legal situation was unclear. Both parties sought protection—the Ennebergers from their bishop, and the nuns from their protector, the duke. Into this situation entered the bishop's call for reform.

The nuns published a protest against Cusanus's reform, characterizing his work as "dictated by hate." In order to discredit any effort of the bishop a priori, no matter how earnest, they wrongfully accused him of acting out of unethical motives, and they explicitly placed themselves under the protection of the duke. In contrast, Nicholas sought to separate the two issues, Enneberg and reform. Despite vigorous resistance the visitation by Bernhard von Waging, prior at Tegernsee, and Michael von Natz, vicar-general to the bishop, took place on November 27, 1453. Bernhard suggested to his friend, Nicholas, that the only remedy for Sonnenburg was to bring in new nuns. He recommended the transfer of three or four sisters from St. Peter's in Salzburg. Under the leadership of their abbess, Verena von Stuben, the Sonnenburg nuns mounted stiff opposition. Using all possible means the abbess plotted against the bishop, incited the other convents to resist and urged the duke to intervene, either directly or through their relatives in the nobility.

In early April 1458, armed men, under orders from Verena von Stuben, attempted to force the farmers of Enneberg, Wengen, and Abtei to pay their fees. This confrontation went forward despite the intervention of ducal advisors who were spending some days with the abbess. The action contradicted agreements with the prince and provincial diets. The abbess was usurping rights that belonged only to the protector or territorial rulers. She was openly breaching the public peace. The farmers who were attacked put up resistance. With an avalanche of stones they dispersed the mass of armed men. Fifty farmhands lay dead. The farmers immediately called on Cusanus's captain, Gabriel Prack, for help. In a counterattack he pressed forward as far as the Sonnenburg convent, but its conquest did not ensue.

No doubt it was above all the later incitement of Gregor Heimburg that caused Cusanus to be railed at as the one guilty of the "murder at Enneberg." It cannot be proven that Cusanus gave Prack the order to intervene. Nevertheless, from a legal standpoint he had every reason to grant approval after the fact to his captain's move against those who had broken the peace. The surprising result of the event was that Duke Sigismund backed off after all and committed himself to work towards Verena's resignation. Although she kept hesitating for half a year, on April 17, 1459, agreement was finally reached through the mediation of the bishop of Trent. On behalf of Cusanus, who was spending some time in Rome, Michael von Natz installed Barbara Schöndorffer as the new abbess. Despite this, it appears as though Verena retained the right to continue living at Sonnenburg.

Sigismund's motives for giving in are unclear. It almost appears as though Verena had become tired of her office. Would it not have been natural for Cusanus to attribute the success to his firmness, even though blood was shed, and even though, as we know, he regretted the bloodshed very much? Yet, did not the bloodshed represent the ultimate consequence of the church's secular rule? Did not war, as the last resort of politics, pose a threat to the church that was supposed to bring peace on earth, not war?

Cusanus believed that he was obligated to preserve undiminished the secular rights of his church in Brixen, and even to regain for it what had been lost. However, in the action at Enneberg a certain overconfidence of the governing prince-bishop emerged when he tested historical necessity despite the danger that needed to be a part of the calculation. In doing this he became entangled in the entire web of difficulties that arose from the secular power of the church.

Personally, he would have given up Brixen if he had been sure that his successor would defend the rights of his church with the same passion as he. During these years when Trent was to be occupied anew, and moreover, the Trent bishopric was threatened with secularization, Cusanus broke out in tears at the thought of the fate facing his neighboring church. If he stood firm in Brixen, it was perhaps in the hope that resoluteness could lead to success for his neighboring bishopric as well. However, he continually received complaints from his bishopric about the spiritual needs of his believers. Robbed of all **means of grace** by the interdict, they turned to their bishop for help. Dark clouds descended on him. The great honors that his last years at the Curia had brought him lost the luster they were intended to have.

Called to Rome

At the end of 1458 when Pius II was preparing to depart for Mantua, he wished to have Nicholas of Cusa as his representative in the administration of the **Papal States**. On January 11, 1459, he appointed Cusanus legate and vicar-general for the secular properties and possessions, and Rome and the provinces on the west side of the Apennines were placed under him. Nicholas applied himself with skill to the political questions of the day that concerned the Papal States. Peace was disturbed by the arguments amongst the vassals of the church when they were not otherwise busy holding out their hand for authority in the Papal States. The legate's attention was occupied first of all by the fighting that took place before the gates of Rome between Everso of Anguillara and the Lords of Vico. When Everso, after an initial attempt at a settlement, launched a surprise attack on the Caprarola Fortress on June 6, Nicholas immediately had it occupied.

The Neapolitan question demanded attention. It involved the Duchy of Anjou that, hostile to the pope and opposed to the Bastard King Ferrante, tried to take power. While the French group in the College of Cardinals worked together with Anjou, Nicholas uncovered a plot in Rome to kill Ferrante. Soon thereafter in Viterbo he safeguarded the church's authority against another surprise attack by Everso. All of these actions made diplomatic intermediaries necessary. For example, thanks to old personal connections, Everso was supported by the Sforzas and the Gonzagas, whom the pope also needed for preparation of the Turkish Crusade. Cusanus was a personal friend of both families.

Furthermore, Nicholas devoted himself to a reorganization of the papal troops, whose activities remained under his direction the entire year. He looked after the revenues, and put down outbreaks of unrest in the city that were stirred up by the Spaniards. The envoy from Milan spoke even of the danger of a "new Sicilian Vespers." The legate devoted himself with the same conscientiousness to the provinces. Again, this meant innumerable details, among them a war between the cities of Rieti and Terni over the water of the Nera River. Only the constant praise of the pope enabled the cardinal to hold out in Rome, for he was burning with desire to find a solution to the Brixen question.

Reform of Rome Fails

Cusanus would have been untrue to himself had he exhausted his energy laboring for the secular well being of the **Patrimony**

of St. Peter (*Patrimonium Sancti Petri*) and not labored for reform. He was the first vicar-general of the Papal States who, in his bull of appointment, was also authorized to reform the Roman clergy. Did these full powers of authority go back to his own initiative?

His calling of a synod to be held on February 10, 1459, for reform of the Roman clergy shows how quickly he went to work. The members of the Curia also participated. In his opening address Cusanus referred to the international character of the synod. As early as January 27 he had begun reforms at the Chapter of St. Peter; on February 23 at St. John in Lateran; and on March 6 at St. Mary Major. Whereas the pope praised Cusanus's reforming zeal, members of the Curia naturally did not respond favorably. Cusanus worked out detailed reform recommendations for the **Roman Rota**, and lastly, he composed a *General Reform of the Church* (*Reformatio generalis*, 1459) in which—as far as the extant text indicates—he dealt primarily with reform of the head of the church. In it he submits the pope himself to examination by the inspectors he appointed. Meanwhile, in preparation for the reform of the Curia Pius II had appointed a commission to which Cusanus also belonged.

Even though all this activity enjoyed less than a hint of success it still does not demonstrate inability on the part of the reformer. How could he have hoped to have led the head of the church, along with the Curia, to the saving reform that only later the greatest crisis of the church could dictate when schism divided the faith? Cusanus, in entertaining this hope, was again presumptuous, and then out of the inevitable failure grew a deep pessimism that overcame him. When the pope took him to task for his ill humor, Cusanus told him to his face: "They don't listen to me when I urge them to do what is right."

Nevertheless, even though it was impossible to renew the whole, Cusanus never spurned the opportunity to act in an indi-

vidual case or on a small scale. Whenever difficult religious matters were brought to the Curia the pope turned them over to his
German friend who could usually handle them successfully. Cusanus's reputation as a theologian ranked alongside that of Cardinal Torquemada, the leading theologian of the Sacred College of
Cardinals. Responding to a controversy between the Dominicans
and Franciscans in Rome at the end of 1462, Cusanus drafted as a
position paper for the pope a thesis and fourteen points about the
hypostatic union and the blood of Christ.

Political Frustrations and the
Congress of Mantua

At the end of September 1459 Pope Pius permitted Cusanus to
come to Mantua. The pope, who liked to describe himself as Cusanus's pupil, was hoping for help from the German for his grand
program for the West. The Congress of Mantua brought together
the princes of Europe to consolidate their power in order to con-
front the Turkish danger effectively after the fall of Constantinople in 1453. At first glance one might think that the pope's hope in
Cusanus was well founded. However, the cardinal proved to hold
a position that differed widely from the pope's. His view had developed during his experience of the political reality that shattered
his dream of unity again and again. On October 9, 1453 Nicholas
wrote with resignation to Jacob von Sierck: "The Turks are going to thrash us, since I no longer see any possibility of forming a
unified group capable of resisting them. Let us find our refuge in
God, although he is not going to listen to sinners!"

Even before the repeat assignment to the English legation in
1455, Nicholas V had entrusted Cusanus with a legation to Prussia
in 1454. The purpose was to negotiate a peace settlement between
the German Order and the Prussian estates. Again, Cusanus saw
the seemingly local question in the whole European context and

characterized the settlement of the Prussian dispute as necessary in view of the Turkish danger. Initially ready to travel, he refrained from going when he recognized that the bull for the legation, taking into consideration other political relationships, had withdrawn the King of Poland from the work of legation even though the king stood with his influence on the side of the Prussian estates.

During his Roman legation, Cusanus pressed the pope with all means available to give up the Congress of Mantua in order to avoid a useless waste of energy that he thought would be better spent within the church itself. Pope Pius had set his highest hopes on the appearance of the emperor. Nicholas doubted whether even princes would come. On March 30, 1459 he convened a gathering of Roman citizens and officials. They were to convince the pope, who had left for Mantua, to turn back since the emperor had cancelled his plans to go. However, the Romans answered the cardinal that since the pope had already departed with the firm intention of holding the Congress in Mantua, and since the Congress had to do with the general welfare of all Christians, they, of all people, did not want to discourage him or confuse him with inappropriate requests.

Cusanus then seemed to contradict his position through his activity as protector of new orders of knights as well as through his role at the Congress as the tireless negotiator and promoter of Pope Pius's plans. The contradiction reveals itself as the conflict between his awareness of the necessity for western unity and the dreadful recognition of political reality.

Nicholas did not shrink from taking this reality into account. An event in 1461 illuminates the situation extremely well. Political circumstances were miserable. The war over the heir to Naples was taking up more and more of the Curia's time. On the other side of the Alps, inflamed by Gregor Heimburg, opposition to the council arose. Archduke Albert went to war against the emperor, who was his brother. Then, on July 22, Charles VII of France died. The Dauphin, Louis XI, who returned from exile, had promised Pius support for the Turkish crusade if he should attain the throne. Cusanus suggested to the pope that they should send the crusade banner to King Louis and offer him a council at Mantua in order to pave the way for the crusade and to reform the church. They thought that Louis, said to be ambitious, would accept. Perhaps they would obtain the repeal of the Pragmatic Sanction of Bourges in return for the pope's break with Ferrante, and much in God's church would be reformed.

Vision versus Reality

Let us remind ourselves of the functions that Cusanus once assigned to the emperor in Christendom: protecting the church from the outside, and ensuring order within through the right to call a council. Now this role went to the king of France, one of the European monarchs in the interplay of political antagonists. Yet not only in this instance did Cusanus see the obvious consequences that come from the reality of the plurality of nations.

For another of Cusanus's entanglements let us recall the importance of the College of Cardinals as the representative body of the church through its members from the various ecclesiatical provinces. Nicholas's *General Reform of the Church* of 1459 attaches critical importance to the cardinals. They are to be the "hinges" (*cardines*) of the church. However, they are no longer representatives of the provinces (*legati provinciarum*), but rather of the nations (*legati nationum*). To be sure, Nicholas was quick to recognize the danger a national cardinal would mean if he were only the executor of a ruler's will. The cardinals had to be independent. So at the end of 1461 Nicholas applied all his energy to oppose the elevation to cardinal of the Bishop of Arras, Jean Jouffroy, because Jouffroy, who did not possess the personal merit for the office, understood his nomination to be a reward for lifting the Pragmatic Sanction. Yet for the same position of cardinal the Gonzaga family had Cusanus enlist the Margrave of Mantua to be the promoter of their son, Francesco. Francesco's mother, Barbara Gonzaga, a niece of Albert Achilles of Brandenburg, was particularly close to Nicholas. Although the personal qualities of the eighteen-year-old Gonzaga scarcely surpassed the merits of the Frenchman, Nicholas backed him without reservation.

Now and then the intractable disparity between theory and practice, concept and reality, led to strange consequences. In 1460 Nicholas wrote to the Salzburg Chancellor, Bernhard von Krayburg: "If through their disobedience priests make themselves unworthy of the protection of the Apostolic See, the time will come when the pope will forsake them and take the side of the opponents of ecclesiastical freedom so that with their assistance he can compel the priests to obey." He continues, however: "I write this with great sorrow, convinced that the kingdom of the church must be completely dissolved because it is inwardly divided, and I have absolutely no hope of changing anything through my recommendations, because I know they are imparted to stubborn people, each one looking only for his own advantage."

Line by line we get a deeper look into the pessimism that was settling over the old cardinal. Nevertheless, Nicholas never threw off the burden of responsibility. Even as bitter blows struck the western world he spoke of his belief in the great "concordance" of all people that would eventually prevail as the fulfillment of humanity. Constantinople had fallen in 1453. If this event were able to call forth only one positive reaction from those who were committed to western unity it was the determination to resist.

Different it was for Cusanus in the treatise he wrote at that time, *The Peace of Faith* (*De pace fidei,* 1453). In it representatives of all nations and religions come together before Christ for a conversation in which they discuss the differences and commonalities in their faiths. The conversation reveals that all of them are enfolded (*complicite*) together, true religion underlies all of them, and they all have a share in it, albeit to differing degrees. Of course, Christianity surpasses the other religions through possession of the complete truth that is imparted only through God's revelation. Yet the task has been set before everyone to exercise devout rivalry in strengthening and purifying one's life in faith and leading it toward perfection. In defining the tension between oneness and multiplicity that arose here Cusanus found the formula of "one religion in the diversity of rites" (*una religio in rituum varietate*).

The work he composed in 1461, *Sifting the Qur'an* (*Cribratio Alkoran*) presents similar thoughts. He wants to show that the Qur'an contains the Christian message of salvation, albeit unclearly and incompletely, but nevertheless in such a way that just "sifting" through the Qur'an could provide the starting-point for conversation. In the same period, Pius II drafted his famous letter to Sultan Mehmed, in which he promised the crown of the eastern empire if the Sultan converted to the Catholic faith. Nicholas goes far beyond these kinds of pragmatic suggestions. He is concerned about spiritual issues that, given the reality of the Islamic religion, require answers.

The Hunt for Wisdom

In his Brixen years as well as now at the Curia where Nicholas is engaged in the service of the entire church, he writes work after work. Almost every year he produces new essays in his "hunt for wisdom" (*De venatione sapientia*), as he calls the treatise he composed in 1462/63. He keeps tackling the fundamental questions of how one is to understand God and the world, and how one is to define oneness and multiplicity and their relationship to each other. Cusanus aids comprehension by using analogies from the realm of experience. For example, he introduces the beryl—the hard, translucent crystal that was sometimes cut for use as a monocle—in order to demonstrate the mysteries of the coincidence of opposites. The mysteries are demonstrated by means of the insights of rational thinking, insights that go beyond conventional wisdom. In *The Beryl* (*De beryllo*), an essay composed in 1458, Nicholas explains that if a beryl is ground into both convex and concave shapes it will disclose things to the eye that previously were hidden. He would like his method to lead in a similar way to knowledge that up to then had been undisclosed.

Nicholas keeps trying different approaches in order to penetrate the mysteries of the divine being. Three of these—we mention only the titles—are *The Vision of God* (*De visione Dei*) of 1453, directed to the monks at Tegernsee, *On Actualized Possibility* (*De possest*) of 1460, and *On the Not-Other* (*De non-aliud*) from the year 1462. Added to these are his mathematical speculations, taken up in the interest of what is universally and eternally true (*sub specie aeternitatis*): *On Complementary Mathematical Considerations* (*De mathematicis complementis*), 1453; *On Squaring the Circle* (*Caesarea circuli quadratura*), 1457; *On Mathematical Perfection* (*De mathematica perfectione*), 1458; and again *The Golden Mean in Mathematics* (*In mathematicis aurea propositio*) of 1459. Recently J. E. Hofmann discovered an unknown early version of *On Mathematical Perfection* in an erased text in a manuscript at Kues. Quantitatively alone Cusanus's mathematical writings take up a significant portion of his entire work, and this does not include the mathematical deliberations in his philosophical treatises. In the latter, as nowhere else, one can see the deep connection between both forms of speculation.

One should not place too much value in Nicholas' mathematical results as such. He lacked sufficient mathematical training. His formulas are often awkward and involved. He did not know about the late scholastic studies down to the *Speculative Geometry* (*Geo-*

metria speculativa) of Thomas Bradwardine. For this reason his independent work is all the more remarkable, especially because he goes beyond the threshold of the "exact." What is new in his way of viewing things, as Hofmann explains, is how he makes perceptible the crossing of the threshold by means of *visio intellectualis,* that is, an intellectual perception. "What Cusanus turns over to the non-mathematical approaches of imagination and inner sensitivities is what, over centuries of struggling with the question, has become the infinitesimal method of modern mathematics."

Nicholas was deceiving himself if he thought a property ascertained in a threshold value sufficed for identifying the law of the construction of numerical order. However, it is not fair to judge him on the basis of whether he was right or wrong, but on the basis of the possibilities for development contained in his ideas. Seen in this way, he takes his place in the history of the development of the function concept and infinitesimal approximation. On the one hand, he illuminates mathematics with basic philosophical-theological insights, while on the other hand he uses the mathematical world for philosophical-theological understanding, with the result that each penetrates the other.

However, at this point the mysteries of faith again lead Nicholas to his deepest insights, as he goes beyond all speculation using the assistance of mathematics and geometry, leaving behind the realm of mortal understanding. On June 5, 1463, he installed a **novice** at the Monte Oliveto monastery in Tuscany, where he preached the sermon. Six days later he expanded on the sermon in a letter to the novice, in which we can see the legacy of Cusanus's thought. The letter, culminating in his latest insights about death, summarizes with consummate wisdom the efforts of his earlier works. The letter teaches us that Nicholas understood the metaphysical location of the universe, its spatial and temporal endlessness in terms of forward-pointing dynamics. We also learn from the letter that

Nicholas recognized the significance of mathematical inquiry and physical measurement, and that he assigned to the human being as a rational creature a place that up to then had not been granted. Yet, all science, in developing its new, future-oriented perspectives, is always encompassed by the higher reality of the Triune God whose image shines forth everywhere. One might dismiss this formulation as a child of its time, but whoever has the solution to this puzzle should make it known.

Return to the Curia

After the debacle at Bruneck Nicholas returned to the Curia to stay for good, and for four more years he applied himself as curial cardinal to the tasks of the universal church. We see an unmistakable reduction in his energy as he carries out a great variety of matters assigned to him by Pius II. The range of tasks is astonishing. They reach across the entire expanse of the western church, from Spain to Sweden, from France to Poland. German and Italian problems stood in the foreground.

Nicholas lived in the palace of the pope, who took care of his living expenses. Now and then the adroit humanist made a little fun of the German, but he placed deep confidence in him in all matters. We will never know to what extent Pius's policies can be credited to Cusanus, but we know that he had private conversations with Cusanus on every important issue. Naturally, we can wonder how much influence Nicholas was able to bring to bear, for despite being close to the pope he was only one individual tied to the College of Cardinals.

In Rome Nicholas enjoyed the highest esteem. In the public eye Sigismund's use of force made Nicholas—despite his quickly forgotten failure—a martyr for the freedom of the church. Vespasiano de Bisticci placed Cusanus in his *Illustrious Men* (*Uomini Illustri*), the hall of fame for the literary greats of his day: "He disdained pomp and circumstance entirely. He was the poorest of cardinals, working hard with no care for reward. He led a life of holiness and gave us the best example in his deeds."

Other Italian writers of the day reported in similar fashion. Voices of those close to the cardinal expressed the same sentiment. The testimony of the envoy from Milan: "I have never seen a better person of greater merit." The representative of Mantua: "In the College of Cardinals he is respected as the mirror and lamp of holiness." A few days after Cusanus's death, the envoy of Breslau: "He was the crown of justice and many other virtues"—and the envoy made the lofty suggestion "that he is holy before God."

Does not the excessive praise cause us to be skeptical? However, we find it repeated in numerous other reports. Frederick van Heiloo of the Netherlands recounts the impression the legate made on him in 1451. He notes Cusanus's tall stature and powerful figure. He finds his face somewhat severe. He says that Cusanus was simple and straightforward in disposition, above all filled with spiritual earnestness. The Dutch chronicler considered it worth noting that Nicholas began his day with his breviary and devotional reading. Similarly, the chronicle of the Monte Oliveto monastery reports with surprise that when the cardinal visited in 1463 he celebrated Holy Mass daily, unlike other cardinals who visited the monastery in those days. In a time of spiritual decay Nicholas of Cusa carried out the duties of a priest day after day.

During these years the lavish endowment income was for the most part withheld from Nicholas. Sigismund had laid his hands on it. Thus it was that in Rome Nicholas was considered a "poor" cardinal. Support came from all sides, especially from friends in the College of Cardinals. Malicious tongues asserted that he replaced the glow of candles with the dull light of oil lamps not out of necessity, but out of stinginess. However, we discover sufficient examples of frugality that are as simple as they are unforced, and these are the best testimonial on his behalf. In 1460 when the Sienese envoy in Mantua arranged lodging for the cardinals who were to travel to Siena he had to take into account the most demanding expectations. Above all, none of them wanted to stay in a cloister. This did not bother Cusanus. He was immediately satisfied to stay at the convent of the Humiliati, which happened to be the first cloister the envoy recommended to him.

On the other hand, Cusanus did not bear his lack of means without complaint. He knew how to secure many an offer of support by continually pointing out his poverty. Yet he made only sparing use of the possibility of having the pope provide him with new benefices. In 1463 he received the provostship of Saint Mauritius in Hildesheim which had already been awarded to Simon von Wehlen in 1460. Neither of them ever came into possession of the benefice. In 1463 Pope Pius assigned Cusanus the prebend of the abbey of San Severo and Martirio near Orvieto. Nicholas owed this to his friendship with his fellow cardinal, Pietro Barbo, who up until that time had held the abbey as a prebend.

Friends and Admirers in Rome

The mention of Barbo directs our attention to the circle of friends and admirers who were around Nicholas in Rome. Along with the pope and Cardinal Barbo, we must mention the Cardinals Bessarion and Carvajal; Antonio Cerdá y Llossos to whom Nicholas dedicated *On the Perfection of Mathematics (De mathematica perfectione)* in early October 1458; Francesco Todeschini-Piccolomini, the pope's nephew and later Pope Pius III, who possessed copies of *The Catholic Concordance* and *General Reformation,* and at a **consistory** as late as 1493 used the example of Nicholas of Cusa to illustrate the steadfastness of a cardinal in obedience to the Holy See. Nicholas named Barbo, Carvajal, and Cardinal Berardo Eroli to be his executors.

Numerous scholars sought the company of the famous German. Especially eager was the humanist Giovanni Andrea Bussi, who promoted the introduction of the printing press in Italy. Nicholas, so he tells, valued this craft very highly and wanted to see it spread throughout Italy. Bussi composed one of the reports in which the Italian public was informed about the events in Bruneck. The addressee was Gaspar Biondo, son of the famous Flavio Biondo, whose *Rome As It Once Appeared* (*Roma instaurata*) and *Italy Described* (*Italia illustrata*) with commentaries by Gaspar became a part of the cardinal's library. He took Gaspar into his close circle of associates. Bussi arranged for Cusanus to meet the Italian humanists Francesco Filelfo and Pietro Balbi.

The Portuguese Fernando Martini de Roriz stayed with the cardinal as personal physician. He was a friend of Toscanelli. Perhaps the minor men of letters, with a desire similar to that of the young Nicholas Treverensis years before, held hopes for favor from the influential cardinal. Cusanus zealously looked after the material well-being of his staff. A special favor of the pope allowed him to determine freely the disposition of his benefices so that after his death they would pass on to his associates.

Rest, Reform, and Reaction in Orvieto

The reference to the wealthy Venetian Cardinal Pietro Barbo, and his gift of letting the pope transfer to Nicholas his prebend of the abbey of San Severo and Martirio, near the town of Orvieto, turns our attention to that town. Beginning in 1461 Cusanus was struck by a life-threatening illness. In addition to eye trouble, he began to have internal pain—intestinal gout that resulted in indigestion and colic-like cramps. This led to the first crisis in June 1461. On June 15 he wrote his first will, but he recovered. However, gout in his hands and feet plagued him to the end of his life. The pain was often so great that he was incapable of any intellectual activity.

Barbo had recommended the town of Orvieto to the conva-
lescing Cusanus. It is located in the refreshing climate of a high,
flat summit above almost vertical cliffs on the northern border of
the Papal States. Barbo himself withdrew to Orvieto during the
hot summer months. Carvajal, too, had stayed there in 1462 as
guest of the wealthy Venetian. Barbo took great pleasure in being
able to extend his patron-like favor to the famous German and to
the Spaniard who had returned from a mission in Hungary that
had required great sacrifice.

From 1461 to 1463 Nicholas spent his summers in Orvieto, but
the location became more than a health resort. After he had been
in town for two weeks a papal communiqué reached the citizens
with the announcement that the cardinal, along with the papal
governor, would look after peace and order in Orvieto. In other
words, Nicholas immediately has another assignment. He is back
into action again! The domestic unrest that afflicted Orvieto, like
almost all other cities, persisted for years. Through energetic intervention, Nicholas was successful as a negotiator in the conflict between the Monaldeschis and Cervaras in a way that met with the
approval of a majority of the citizens in Orvieto. Soon, however,
these political questions took a back seat to the assignment that
the pope—certainly following Cusanus's own wish—bestowed on
him in 1463, appointing him inspector and reformer of the town
and diocese.

Before his eyes stood the great possibility of creating in Orvieto a model church and town over which he himself, as the responsible governor, would preside. They would be purified through
reform and correspond to his ideals. He plunged into the final
reform work of his life! Prospects looked good, since the citizens
had been satisfied by the way in which he had settled the political
discord. He was deceiving himself, however. Reform meant sacrifice, restrictions, firmness. All his efforts ran up against the same

obstacle that had so often blocked his path. He was enmeshed in relationships with the influential families of the town who had provided very well for their relatives in Orvieto's monasteries and convents, and who, with massive support from the citizenry, resisted reform.

Although Nicholas proceeded in a well-considered manner, reforming first the cathedral church and intending to follow up with reform of the other churches, opposition was sparked right away by the planned merging of all municipal hospices with the cathedral hospital. In an emotional speech the official representative of the town reminded the cardinal that one needed to respect the will of the donors to whom the hospices owed their existence. The cardinal had no success with his argument that due to their small size the facilities offered no guarantee of fruitful work, while centralization could better eliminate the well-entrenched deficiencies.

Since his departure for Rome was imminent, Nicholas had to act under the pressure of time. Knowing this full well, the people of Orvieto deliberately dragged their feet. Nicholas transferred the continuation of his work to a Carmelite, Gaspar de Sicilia. This appointment proved to be a complete mistake. The people of Orvieto had good reason to complain about Gaspar's youthful inexperience. When he ventured to interfere with the prior of the Servite Order in Orvieto the city turned to the cardinal with its complaint, but the complainants were no longer able to reach him in Rome.

Final Illness and Death

In the summer of 1464 the great wish of Pope Pius II was finally realized. The crusade began! Since the princes balked, the pope placed himself at the head of the crusaders. At his call more riff-raff than useful warriors came together in Italy from all over Europe. At the end of June Pius II set off from Rome for Ancona in excruciating heat and also under great hardship, since he was near death. At Ancona the Venetian fleet was to take the army on board.

Nicholas was instructed to gather up the "knights of the crusade," whose number was estimated to be 5,000 or more. They were wandering between Ancona and Rome, dying like flies under the blazing sun. Nicholas left the Eternal City prior to July 3, 1464. We do not know whether he was able to fulfill his assignment. On July 16 we find him lying sick in the little Umbrian mountain town of Todi. It is here that the representatives from Orvieto met him. Nicholas lamented his own physical misery, but what of any substance was he to say about the charges brought against Gaspar? Deep resignation fills his last letter, one he directed to the people of Orvieto: "You know well how difficult it is to find a person who knows how to govern without reproach." Then he admonishes the city "to keep its composure so that no trouble arises." His final advice: "Maintain your peace and quiet and pray earnestly to God, as do we, that he might free you from the present ills."

On July 28 the archbishop of Milan reported from Ancona to Francesco Sforza, Duke of Milan, that the cardinal was suffering from such a high fever that he was giving up hope for him. On August 6 Cusanus drew up a new will. On August 11 he died. His papal friend, Aeneas Sylvius, followed him in death three days later. This Italian humanist was granted one emotional closing scene, the finale of Ancona, as he passed away with his eyes on the incoming Venetian fleet. Meanwhile, in the Umbrian mountains, half-way to his destination, without any drama, without supporting actors, in a small circle of relatives and friends—those named are Toscanelli, Bussi, Roriz, Johann Römer, Peter of Erkelenz— his final disappointment behind him, the cardinal died—the bishop, the great scholar, Cusanus, Treverensis, Nichlaß von Cuße, Krebshenne's son.

Burial

Cusanus's body was brought to Rome immediately and laid to rest in his titular church. "He loved God, feared and worshiped him, and served him alone. The promise of the reward has not failed him." To this inscription for his gravestone he added his specific wish to be buried near the chains of St. Peter. Nicholas's admiration for St. Peter is expressed by the **distich** composed by Giovanni Andrea Bussi that is on the monument erected in the year following his death. In triptychlike form the monument portrays St. Peter in the middle, flanked on one side by the angel who freed him from his chains, and on the other side by the kneeling cardinal. Nicholas wanted to be sure that posterity knew he had served the Chair of St. Peter. To find Nicholas's original gravesite one would look in the immediate vicinity of the chains, but undoubtedly his grave was moved when the church was renovated under Sixtus IV and Julius II, who as cardinals were Nicholas's immediate successors at St. Peter in Chains. No gravesite has been discovered where today the gravestone and monument are located in the left side aisle.

We are uncertain whether we can attribute the first-rate, high relief on the monument to Andrea Bregno. The work is definitely Lombardian, yet it is less refined and at the same time more expressive than the artist's typical works. With an empathetic spirit Edmond Vansteenberghe, the great Cusanus biographer, pondered deeply the figure and countenance of the cardinal on the monument. We do not know of any words that match those of Vansteenberghe: "We see the 'great,' the 'handsome' man in the prime of life, yet already bent, more from work and the trials and tribulations of life than from the burdens of age. Yet the physical beauty lives on in the beauty of the heart that shimmers over his features like a soft light. The eyes—sympathetic, yielding to resignation, and yet without sadness! We stop before this figure, surprised by the dignity, seized by the beauty! The expression, breathing a firm and calm confidence, yet conscious of the un-avoidability of evil! He is through and through the long-suffering one who nevertheless has faith and love, who never harvested but only sowed, and yet knew of the fruitfulness of his work, who re-mained optimistic in spite of all disappointments, setting his entire hope on a better world—the world beyond."

The portrait of Cusanus on the winged altar in the hospital chapel at Kues makes it clear that the figure on the monument is modeled after the real life person. It could almost remind us of a mask that is used as an aid. At first the altar portrait appears nar-rower, more elongated, not as stocky as the head and figure on the monument. If, like using the eye of the photographer, we view the monument from the same perspective as that of the altar painting, then the monument depicts the cardinal as older, more wrinkled, almost as though his life is already ebbing away. His face appears even more serious. The faint smile has disappeared from his lips.

The Hospital in Kues

In accordance with Cusanus's wish his heart was laid to rest not in Rome, but in Kues. The site is in the hospital chapel. In 1488 Peter of Erkelenz had the location covered with a bronze plaque modeled after the gravestone in Rome. If anywhere the hope has been fulfilled that the seed Cusanus sowed would bear fruit, it is here, for the hospital in Kues has lived on in the spirit of service for more than 500 years.'

When, on December 3, 1458, Cusanus prepared the document establishing the hospital he made thorough provision for the in-stitution's material well-being. Creating the hospital gave him the opportunity to test his skill in such things and see if he could suc-ceed. Not only did the large assets of the family flow into the in-

FIGURE 8. St. Nicholas Hospital today, on the banks of the Mosel River in Kues.

stitution, but also the periodic, truly "princely" income from his offices in the church. It was to be used for devout purposes, for loving service and Christian deeds. Thirty-three poor, work-worn old men were to find their final home at the institution. They promised chastity, obedience, and faithfulness, wore an entirely grey garment, and followed a common, daily schedule. Out of understanding for their old age the rules were relaxed. Their number reminded them daily of the example of the one who for thirty-three years walked on earth as God and human being.

The hospital houses a unique intellectual treasure: the cardinal's library. While many manuscripts got away—numerous ones are found today in Brussels and, above all, in London—the library contains not only the treasure of his books but also other items that have been preserved, such as his astronomical instruments.

The vaulted, gothic room that looks out toward the banks of the Mosel breathes like no other place the spirit of Cusanus, even though he himself never entered it. The visitor should definitely not miss opening the little window in the niche at the rear corner that affords a view into the chapel. There, where Cusanus's heart rests, the church stands at the heart of the extensive complex. His intellectual legacy is kept directly next to the church, physically connected to it and, as it were, leading to it.

The vaulting of the square main room unfolds from one middle pillar that bears everything; the three-bay chancel with walls on three sides opens to the east. We are quite certain that the con-

FIGURE 9. The library of Cusanus's works and artifacts in St. Nicholas Hospital, Kues.

cept for the construction of the chapel and hospital goes back to Cusanus. We do not know what models he had in mind, or which ones the builders—perhaps Bohemian or Southern German—suggested. Readers of his works are free to let the chapel's architecture inspire them to interpret its symbolism.

Legacy

The generations following Cusanus, while searching for accomplices in their own intellectual forays, have wanted to uncover in him the one whose thought is related to theirs. Often enough their one-sidedness has led them to misinterpret Cusanus and this, in turn, has done harm to his reputation, until he was even reputed to have been a liberal heretic. Some, searching in an overly critical manner, have discovered "medieval superstition" in him and eventually have thought one can do justice to his achievements only with apologetic, compromising assessments. In particular, nonconformists of all types have claimed Cusanus, some deliberately, while others have unexpectedly picked up something from him.

He was one of the greatest thinkers of his time, yet he formed no school, even though he had many admirers. He belonged to no order or university that could have provided the organizational structure for a school. He was so original, so individual, so one-of-a-kind. These traits became, of course, equally characteristic for the age of the Renaissance, which was just beginning, and they lead us to think of other personalities like Leonardo, Galileo, Spinoza, and Leibniz.

In Meier-Oeser's phrase, "the presence of the forgotten" in succeeding centuries has long been underestimated, but enough material about how Cusanus lives on can be gathered together to fill entire books. The actual rediscovery of Cusanus has, of course, been reserved for our century, perhaps because with its problems our age really is not so far removed from that of Cusanus.

Cusanus, standing between two ages—so we can say today—not only connected them, not only led the old into the new, not only broke up the old for the new, but mastered both with a unique, scarcely repeatable achievement. We have looked not only for what the man did, but we have tried to discover the man behind it. We wanted to perceive in the man himself the roots of his thinking, the starting-points of his thought.

"It is a great thing to root oneself firmly in the union of opposites," he wrote at the end of his life in his work about the beryl. He experienced this tension between opposites every single day, and he knew they were not to be reconciled only by taking off in flights of speculative thought. Upon the down-to-earth, firm ground of this insight into things grew the concept that the freedom of contracted humanity (*humanitas contracta*) can advance only as far as an approximation of the goal of absolute humanity (*humanitas absoluta*), until it is taken into the perfection of grace. Only from this standpoint of grace can one understand all human activity. "The Word of God," he once preached, "has sent out everyone, so to a certain extent we are talking about a sending of everyone, that there is one who sends and many who are sent who follow him and receive the reward of his sending." A contemporary of Cusanus believed he could scoff at him, "He who first has taken from many can then easily give to others." Certainly, this belittler did not recognize the dilemma of the man who did not step before the world modestly, yet a world that hardly would have disclosed its essence to him so clearly had he not experienced the world in his own failings.

He was not one of those great sinners whom we can turn into a romantic hero through the dialectic of fall and redemption. By recognizing his own weakness—in which he could face his doubts about whether he had made the right decisions with only the same advice he gave to the people of Orvieto, "Keep your composure!"—he approaches us not only as a philosopher but, above all, as a human being. There lie the deepest reasons for his longing for concordance and coincidence, tempered by his understanding of reality, an understanding represented in the mind as the asymptotic nature of all mortal striving, of having to persist toward degrees of approximation.

Often we have used the word "effort." Perhaps a wise lesson lies herein, because he lived a life of effort, not excess. He was obsessed with the "hunt for wisdom" as well as with the drive to get things done. In the one as well as the other, he finally found rest in what was for him the last possible coincidence, in grace, by means of which we all conquer in Christ and possess God. "And this possessing God merges through Christ with being possessed by God. Here Christ's mediation reveals its true meaning. It forms the connecting link for the coincidence between the ascent of the inner human being to God and the descent of God to the human being."

In nothing more than this coincidence his "legation" was fulfilled.

Glossary

ABBESS

The superior in a community of nuns.

ABBOT

The superior in a community of monks.

ABBREVIATOR

An official in the papal curia who wrote out the bulls, letters, and decrees in their official form; so named because of the use of abbreviations to reduce the amount of writing.

BENEFICE

Refers to a source of income or the income itself assigned to a cleric of whatever rank, the revenue coming from a property (often land), parish church, an institution, endowment from an altar or chapel, or even from patronage. The principle was that the cleric received revenue ("temporalities") in return for performing pastoral duties ("spiritualities"). A cleric could hold multiple benefices.

BRETHREN OF THE COMMON LIFE

Geert de Groote (1340–1384), born in Deventer in the Netherlands, renounced his ecclesiastical career and with a stirring message of reform inspired great numbers, including a band of young men who gathered around him to form (ca. 1381) the first "Brethren of the Common Life." Communities of predominantly laymen and laywomen that grew from this took no vows, cultivated the spiritual life, promoted literature and education, and are known for having inspired the Modern Devotion (*devotio moderna*). This form of piety led to a second type of community, the Windesheim Congregation.

BREVIARY

A liturgical book (from Latin *brevis,* "concise") that contains the lessons, prayers, hymns, and Psalms for use in the Office, i.e., the "hours" of worship throughout the day and night.

BULL (PAPAL BULL, BULL OF SUBMISSION, ETC.)

A letter containing a solemn pronouncement by the pope, the term derived from the Latin *bulla,* or "leaden seal," since the letters were traditionally sealed with lead.

CANON

In Cusanus's time a priest who belonged to the permanent staff of a cathedral or collegiate church, lived with others in the vicinity of the cathedral or church, often followed a rule, and was responsible for maintaining the building and liturgical services. See also *Collegiate Chapter.*

CANON LAW

The body of regulations that governs the church. Its main sources are the Bible, decrees of the councils, the *Decretum* of Gratian (ca. 1144) and papal declarations known as "decretals."

CANONS REGULAR

Those canons who live under a rule, especially the Augustinian Canons who follow the Rule of Augustine.

COLLEGIATE CHAPTER

"Collegiate" refers to the "college," or group of priests, that oversees worship in a particular church. Members are called "canons" and live together in a "chapter." A cathedral chapter, as distinguished from a collegiate chapter, serves, as the name indicates, a cathedral.

CONCORDAT

A formal agreement or treaty between the papacy and a temporal authority or state.

CONGREGATION (WINDESHEIM CONGREGATION)

A group of monasteries and/or convents affiliated with one another through choosing to follow the same rule, and by maintaining contact through, for example, an annual meeting of representatives from the cloisters. A cloister founded in Windesheim in 1387 initiated the congregation that in 1430 encompassed thirty-one cloisters in the Netherlands and Germany.

CONSISTORY

In general, an ecclesiastical court, where, for example, a bishop administers justice for his diocese. In particular, it is the meeting of the pope and cardinals to receive ambassadors, install new cardinals, and conduct other business.

CURIA

A group of ecclesiastical officials who assist in the governance of the church, ranging from the relatively simple diocesan curia to the larger patriarchal curias to the Roman Curia, which assists the pope in governing the entire Roman Catholic Church.

DEANERY

The office of a dean, one who has supervisory duties for a number of parishes grouped together in a prescribed, normally rural, area. The dean ranks close to the bishop.

DECRETALS

Papal letters enunciating ecclesiastical decisions with the force of law. After Gratian had collected canon law in his *Decretum,* around 1144, popes began to publish collections of these decretals, which, together with the decisions of the councils, are chief sources of the legislation of the church.

DISTICH

A couplet, or self-contained two-lined unit of verse.

ENDOWED ALTAR

An altar, as well as the clergy who attended to the prayers or masses at the altar and looked after its care, and even the building necessary to house the altar, all endowed by pious donations to maintain regular use of the altar for its designated purpose, such as prayers for the donor.

FOUNDATION

An institution, typically a monastery, convent, or hospital, founded and/or supported by private endowment or donations. By extension the term can refer to the chapter of cloistered persons themselves.

INTERDICT

A penalty imposed by the church on an individual, group, region, or even country barring the sacraments and participation in public worship. When imposed on a territory it was, for an individual, equivalent to excommunication since it caused all the churches to be closed, thus cutting off almost all sacraments (i.e., marriage, confession, anointing of the sick, and the Eucharist).

JUBILEE YEAR

A holy year proclaimed by the pope during which the church bestowed a special "Jubilee Indulgence" on those who made pilgrimage to Rome. The first holy year was 1300; in 1343 the pope declared that jubilees would recur at fifty year intervals.

LEGATE (PAPAL LEGATE)

A pope's personal representative, often a cardinal with "full authority" (*plena potestas*) sent out by the pope to act on his behalf in important missions.

MAGISTRATE

A judicial officer who hears civil and minor criminal cases or conducts preliminary examinations of these cases; a civil office.

MEANS OF GRACE
The sacraments.

MENDICANT ORDERS
Designation given first to the Franciscans and Dominicans. Taking a vow of poverty, they did not own property, neither individually nor in common. Unlike orders of monks such as the Benedictines who lived in monasteries, mendicants were not required to live in fixed communities, but lived an itinerant life, working and begging for their upkeep.

MODERN DEVOTION
See *Brethren of the Common Life.*

NOVICE
A new member of a monastic community who is in a period of probation.

NUNCIO
A papal representative, generally without the powers of a legate, to a civil government, often on a state level, comparable to a diplomat or envoy today.

PAPAL ORATOR
Representative of the pope but without the authority to take action on his behalf, as is invested in a legate.

PAPAL STATES (PATRIMONY OF ST. PETER)
From 754 to 1870 a collection of independent territories, mostly in central Italy, varying in size at different times, over which the papacy was temporal as well as spiritual sovereign. Also called the States of the Church or Pontifical States.

PATRIMONY OF ST. PETER
See *Papal States.*

POOR CLARES

An order for women founded by Clare (1193?–1253), an Italian nun of Assisi who was devoted to St. Francis, carried on his ideal of poverty, and organized her companions into an order of Franciscan nuns who led a contemplative life.

PRAGMATIC SANCTION OF BOURGES

A declaration by the French clergy issued by Charles VII of France in 1438 that prohibited papal nominations to vacant churches and asserted the right of the church to administer its properties apart from the papacy, thus establishing liberties from papal authority. "Gallicanism" is this tradition of the French church's resistance to the authority of Rome.

PREBEND

A type of benefice, prebend refers to the source of income, or the income itself, assigned to a cleric, and normally derived from a cathedral, usually from its estates. The cleric holding a prebend is a "prebendary." A person could hold multiple prebends.

PRIOR

In a monastery a superior rank, usually one rank lower than the head of the monastery (abbot), but in some cases the head.

PRIOR GENERAL

Superior of more than one community of monks.

PROCURATOR

An agent who is appointed to manage the administrative responsibilities of a bishopric or province.

PROVINCIAL

Provincial councils, synods, etc., were regional assemblies of bishops or their representatives, convened to resolve in their respective dioceses local issues related to church order or doctrine.

PROVOST

The head of a collegiate or cathedral chapter, exercising a high degree of authority in the particular parish, and, in the case of a cathedral, in the diocese; also the title of the official who is second in authority to an abbot in a monastery.

ROMAN ROTA

The pope's desire for advice and counsel in ecclesiastical and civil cases led by the early 1300s to the formation of a high tribunal—named "Rota" because its original members heard cases in a round room—that took on the function of the highest appellate court of the Holy See.

SACRAMENTALS

Aids to devotion that, unlike the sacraments instituted by Christ, do not confer grace in and of themselves, but depend on one's devotion. Commonly divided into six categories: prayer, anointing, eating, confession, giving, and blessing. Examples include making the sign of the cross, statues, incense, and rosaries.

SERVITIA

Shortened reference for *servitia communia* or *servitia Camerae Papae,* the payment into the papal treasury required of every abbot and bishop upon induction into office of one year's revenue of his new benefice; one of three forms of "annates," i.e., the first year's income from a benefice normally given to the papal treasury.

SIMONY

The purchase or sale of sacred things, derived from the story in Acts 8:18–24 in which Simon Magus attempts to buy the power of the Holy Spirit; in the Middle Ages often the buying and selling of church offices.

TITHE

As a contribution of one tenth of the whole, the tithe was a levy or tax on individuals and villages paid to the respective ecclesiastical or civil authority. Payment was not necessarily monetary; farmers often brought one tenth of their harvest to the village "tithe barn."

TITULAR CHURCH
The *tituli* were early churches surrounding Rome, to each of which a cardinal was assigned as an honor and a way of making him a member of the Roman clergy. He thus became a priest or deacon of his "titular" church.

TONSURED
The state of having a "tonsure," i.e., a round, shaved spot often at the crown of the head, most prominent among monks, and a symbol of renouncing worldly fashion.

VICAR
In the broadest sense a vicar is one who acts in place of a superior, such as a bishop. The title of a vicar varies depending on the role that he is performing.

VICAR-GENERAL
The highest-ranking representative of a bishop, authorized to carry out the bishop's executive functions, and thus second-in-command in administration of the diocese.

VISITATION
An inspection, often on a tour to more than one facility, by a bishop or his representative for the purpose of examining the institution's state of affairs, and, as necessary, regulating doctrine and morals.

WINDESHEIM CONGREGATION
See *Brethren of the Common Life; Congregation.*

Bibliographic Notes on
Cusanus Research

The earlier literature is treated in the seminal biography by E. Vansteenberghe, *Le cardinal Nicolas de Cues (1401–1464)*. *L'action— la pensée* (Paris, 1920; unaltered reprints, Frankfurt, 1963, and Geneva, 1974).

The first review of literature appearing after 1920 is in *Mitteilungen und Forschungsbeiträge der Cusanus-Gesellschaft (MFCG)* 1 (Mainz, 1961): 95–126 (411 titles), and the review is continually brought up to date in this series; see *MFCG* 3 (1963): 223–37; 6 (1967): 178–202; 10 (1973): 207–34; and 15 (1982): 121–47.

The critical edition of Cusanus's works is published by the Heidelberg Academy of Sciences (*Heidelberger Akademie der Wissenschaften*): *Nicolai de Cusa Opera omnia. Iussu et auctoritate Academiae Litterarum Heidelbergensis ad codicum fidem edita* (Leipzig-Hamburg: Meiner, 1932–). The *Acta Cusana* has appeared since 1976 in a special series of the Academy edition as the basis for a future biography.

Sermons, tracts, letters, and other documents are edited in the series *Cusanus-Texte* as *Sitzungsberichte der Heidelberger Akademie* (Heidelberg, 1929–). These are also included later in the *Opera omnia*.

For Cusanus's works that have not yet appeared in critical editions, one can consult the *Nicolai Cusae Cardinalis Opera,* ed. Faber Stapulensis (Paris, 1514; unaltered reprint, Frankfurt, 1962). More recent and better: *Nikolaus von Kues. Werke,* using the Strasbourg edition of 1488, newly published by P. Wilpert (Berlin, 1966).

Many writings are available in German translation, a great number of which were commissioned by the Heidelberg Academy: *Schriften des Nikolaus von Cues, im Auftrag der Heidelberger Akademie der Wissenschaften in deutscher Übersetzung.* They appear in the *Philoso-*

phische Bibliothek of the Meiner-Verlag (Leipzig-Hamburg, 1936–). In addition, *Nikolaus von Kues, Philosophisch-theologische Schriften, Studien- und Jubiläumsausgabe,* ed. and introduction by L. Gabriel, translation and commentary by D. and W. Dupré (Vienna, 1964–1967).

Noteworthy is the great number of translations into other languages, above all into Italian (G. Santinello, among others), French, English, and Russian (most recently: Moscow 1979/80, 150,000 copies). In addition, numerous translations of individual works have appeared. Of these, *De concordantia catholica, De docta ignorantia, De visione Dei, De pace fidei* enjoy a particularly lively interest.

G. Heinz-Mohr and W. P. Eckert, *Das Werk des Nicolaus Cusanus* (Cologne, 1981) continues to stand out as a fine introductory work. Complementing this now is the collection, *Zugänge zu Nikolaus von Kues. Festschrift zum 25jährigen Bestehen der Cusanus-Gesellschaft* (Bernkastel-Kues, 1986), ed. H. Gestrich, in cooperation with the Institute for Cusanus Research in Trier. The Cusanus Society, along with being co-sponsor of the Cusanus Institute, regards updating and popularizing the Cusanus legacy as an essential task. Both the Institute and the Society would be unthinkable without the initiative of R. Haubst (d. 1992), who directed the Institute from its founding in 1960. In particular, he guided the edition of the sermons in the Heidelberg Academy collection.

In recent times, H. G. Senger wrote succinct introductions in *Gestalten der Kirchengeschichte* IV, ed. M. Greschat, (Stuttgart, 1983), 287–307, and in *Die deutsche Literatur des Mittelalters. Verfasserlexikon* VI (Berlin, 1987), 1093–113. Several collections oriented toward a more comprehensive presentation appeared on the occasion of the Cusanus Jubilees, for instance *MFCG* 4 (1964) containing the presentations held in Bernkastel-Kues in 1964; the proceedings of the 1964 Brixen Congress published under the title *Nicolò Cusano agli inizi del mondo moderno* (Florence, 1970); as well as the *Cusanus-Gedächtnisschrift,* ed. N. Grass (Innsbruck-Munich, 1970). Contributions of several authors are found in *Nikolaus von Kues. Einführung in sein philosophisches Denken,* ed. K. Jacobi, *Kolleg Philosophie* (Freiburg-Munich, 1979); likewise *Nicholas of Cusa in Search of God and Wisdom: Essays in Honor of Mor-*

imichi Watanabe by the American Cusanus Society, ed. G. Christianson and T. M. Izbicki (Leiden, 1991).

The last-named collection contains an informative account of the "Origins of Modern Cusanus Research in Germany and the Foundation of the Heidelberg *Opera omnia,*" M. Watanabe. For further orientation to the development of research one can consult *MFCG,* of which twenty volumes have appeared up to now (1961–1992). Furthermore, shorter reports of research by H. G. Senger are in *Contemporary Philosophy. A New Survey* VI, no. 1 (Dordrecht-Boston, 1990), 563–603; and H. G. Senger, "Research on Cusanus in America," *The American Cusanus Society Newsletter (ACSN)* VII (1990): 34–44; as well as T. M. Izbicki, "Nicholas of Cusa: The Literature in English through 1988," in *Nicholas of Cusa in Search of God and Wisdom* (see previously), 259–81.

In recent monographs only individual periods of Cusanus's life have been elucidated. E. Meuthen, *Das Trierer Schisma von 1430 auf dem Basler Konzil* (Münster, 1964) (in this connection, H. Heimpel, *Die Vener von Gmünd und Straßburg 1162–1447* [Göttingen, 1982]); J. Koch, *Nikolaus von Cues und seine Umwelt* (Heidelberg, 1948); E. Meuthen, "Die deutsche Legationsreise des Nikolaus von Kues 1451/1452," in *Lebenslehren und Weltentwürfe im Übergang vom Mittelalter zur Neuzeit,* ed. H. Boockmann, B. Moeller, and K. Stackmann (Göttingen, 1989), 421–99; E. Meuthen, *Die letzten Jahre des Nikolaus von Kues* (Cologne-Opladen, 1958); B. Schwarz, "Über Patronage und Klientel in der spätmittelalterlichen Kirche am Beispiel des Nikolaus von Kues," in *Quellen und Forsch. aus ital. Archiven und Bibliotheken* 68 (1988): 284–310. Meanwhile, H. Hallauer has set our knowledge of the Brixen epoch on a new foundation through numerous individual studies. The pertinent titles are named in *Acta Cusana* I, no. 1, VIIIf.; further items most recently in *MFCG* 19 (1991). In addition, see W. Baum, *Nikolaus Cusanus in Tirol* (Bozen, 1983). J. Marx, *Die Geschichte des Armen-Hospitals zum hl. Nikolaus zu Cues* from 1907 has been republished by the Cusanus Society (Bernkastel, 1976).

M. de Gandillac offers a comprehensive assessment of Cusanus's intellectual work, *Nikolaus von Cues* (Düsseldorf, 1953). Also stimulating is S. Schneider, *Die "kosmische" Größe Christi als Ermöglichung seiner universalen Heilswirksamkeit an Hand des kosmogenetischen Entwurfes Teilhard de Chardins und der Christologie des Nikolaus von Kues* (Münster, 1979). Recently, J. Stallmach, *Ineinsfall der Gegensätze und Weisheit des Nichtwissens. Grundzüge der Philosophie des Nikolaus von Kues* (Münster, 1989), appeared as a special contribution in the *Buchreihe der Cusanus-Gesellschaft,* which up to now contains ten regular volumes. The latest: F. Nagel, *Nicolaus Cusanus und die Entstehung der exakten Wissenschaften* (Münster, 1984); and S. Meier-Oeser, *Die Präsenz des Vergessenen. Zur Rezeption des Nicolaus Cusanus vom 15. bis zum 18. Jahrhundert* (Münster, 1989).

The person who has made Cusanus's theology more easily understood is, above all, R. Haubst. See, for example, *Das Bild des Einen and Dreieinen Gottes in der Welt nach Nikolaus von Kues* (Trier, 1952), and *Die Christologie des Nikolaus von Kues* (Freiburg, 1956); finally, serving at the same time as a summary, the collection *Streifzüge in die cusanische Theologie* (Münster, 1991), with a reprint of his numerous essays on Cusanus's theology.

Among others, the following offered important contributions on philosophical and theological subjects: J. Koch, P. Wilpert, M. Álvarez-Gómez, W. Beierwaltes, J. E. Biechler, H. Blumenberg, K. Bormann, G. von Bredow, A. Brüntrup, E. Colomer, E. Cranz, D. F. Duclow, W. Dupré, K. Flasch, H.-G. Gadamer, M. de Gandillac, J. Hopkins, K. Jacobi, R. Klibansky, K. Kremer, W. Lentzen-Deis, H. Meinhardt, P. Moffitt Watts, U. Offermann, S. Oide, T. Sakamoto, G. Santinello, W. Schwarz, H. G. Senger, M. Stadler, J. Stallmach, and K. H. Volkmann-Schluck. Regarding Cusanian mathematics, see the numerous studies by J. E. Hofmann. The exact titles are easily available through the "Cusanus Bibliography" in *MFCG.* The works on Cusanus by J. Koch are reprinted in J. Koch, *Kleine Schriften* I (Rome, 1973).

Cusanus's socio-political theory is treated by G. Heinz-Mohr, *Unitas christiana* (Trier, 1958); M. Watanabe, *The Political Ideas of Nicholas of Cusa* (Geneva, 1963); and above all P. E. Sigmund, *Nicholas of Cusa and Medieval Political Thought* (Cambridge, Mass., 1963). The following serves as an introduction to *The Catholic Concordance*: H. J. Sieben,

"Der Konzilstraktat des Nikolaus von Kues: De concordantia catholica," *Annuarium Historiae Conciliorum* 14 (1982): 171–226. Recently, J. W. Stieber, "The 'Hercules of the Eugenians' at the Crossroads," in *Nicholas of Cusa in Search of God and Wisdom* (see previously), 221–55.

Of the numerous studies about the influences on Cusanus, examples are E. Colomer, *Nikolaus von Kues und Raimund Llull* (Berlin, 1961), and L. Hagemann, *Der Kur'an in Verständnis und Kritik bei Nikolaus von Kues* (Frankfurt, 1976). The *Opera omnia* places special weight on identifying the important sources for Cusanus as well as on his ongoing influence.

From the beginning, Nicholas of Cusa has created interest not only among German scholars but to a remarkable degree among international scholars. In most recent times this interest has become well institutionalized, for example, in Japan with the Japanese Cusanus Society (current president, S. Oide) and, above all, in the United States with the American Cusanus Society (current president, M. Watanabe). Since 1983 the latter has published *The American Cusanus Society Newsletter (ACSN)*, which offers information about activities of the Society.

Bibliographic Notes
on Cusanus Research,
1992–2005

HANS GERHARD SENGER

In the following, NC denotes Nicholas of Cusa;
NvK denotes Nikolaus von Kues.

Editions

Along with *Opera omnia Nicolai de Cusa,* the critical edition mentioned previously, a Latin-German collection, *Nikolaus von Kues, Philosophisch-theologische Werke,* ed. K. Bormann, 4 volumes (Hamburg,
2002), is drawn from the Latin-German study edition, *Schriften des
NvK in deutscher Übersetzung.* J. Hopkins published "all of the major
treatises and dialogues of NC, except for *De concordantia catholica,*" in
English translation with notes, commentaries, and introductory studies: 10 volumes, some already in the second or third edition, all by the
Arthur J. Banning Press (Minneapolis, 1981–2000).

Bibliographies

In *Introducing Nicholas of Cusa: A Guide to a Renaissance Man* (see
"Recent Introductions to Cusanus" following), 409–57, the bibliography compiled by T. M. Izbicki and K. S. Breighner "attempts to list all
published literature in English on NC from Tudor times to the end
of 2002." H. G. Senger offers a report on research in the last fifteen
years, "Cusanus Literatur der Jahre 1986–2001," *Recherches de Théologie
et Philosophie médiévales* 69, no. 1 (2002): 225–42; and its continuation,
69, no. 2 (2002): 371–94. H. G. Senger, *Die Literatur über NvK 1469–2001.
Eine Cusanus-Bibliographie* will appear soon in the *Cusanus-Studien* of

the Philosophical-Historical Division of the Heidelberg Academy of Sciences, Heidelberg.

Biographies

The collection *Acta Cusana. Quellen zur Lebensgeschichte des NvK,* commissioned by the Heidelberg Academy of Sciences, was continued with volume I, facsimile 3a and 3b (January 1451–March 1452), ed. E. Meuthen and H. Hallauer, and contains the records of the legation journey, 1451–1452. This is masterfully expanded by the editor E. Meuthen with facsimile 4: *Literatur und Register zu Bd. I* (Hamburg, 1996 and 2000); together, approximately 1,140 pages. Important for the Brixen period is H. J. Hallauer, *Nikolaus von Kues, Bischof von Brixen 1450–1464,* in *Gesammelte Aufsätze,* ed. E. Meuthen and J. Gelmi, assisted by A. Kaiser, *Veröffentlichungen der Hofburg Brixen* I (Bolzano/Bozen, 2002). M. Watanabe continued his series, begun in 1984, on places associated with Cusanus, "Following Cusanus' Steps" (since 1995, "Footsteps"), in *The American Cusanus Society Newsletter (ACSN)* 9, no. 2 (1992)–21, no. 1 (2004). Likewise the series begun in 1987: "Cusanus' Contemporaries," in *ACSN* 9, no. 1 (1992)–20, no. 2 (2003). Each of these is rich in bibliographical references.

Journals

The periodical *Mitteilungen und Forschungsbeiträge der Cusanus-Gesellschaft (MFCG)* continued with volumes 20–28 (Trier, 1992–2003). Some of the themes are: *Weisheit und Wissenschaft. Cusanus im Blick auf die Gegenwart,* MFCG 20 (1992); *NvK. Kirche und res publica Christiana. Konkordanz, Repräsentaz und Konsens,* MFCG 21 (1994); *Unsterblichkeit und Eschatologie im Denken des NvK,* MFCG 23 (1996); *NvK als Kanonist und Rechtshistoriker,* MFCG 24 (1998); *Sein und Sollen. Die Ethik des NvK,* MFCG 26 (2000). *ACSN* 1, no. 1 (October, 1983)–21, no. 2 (2004). Semi-annual *Bulletin der Japanischen Cusanus-Gesellschaft* 1 (1983)–18 (1992). A new publication is *Litterae Cusanae. Informationen der Cusanus-Gesellschaft,* ed. H. Gestrich and K. Reinhardt, 2, no. 1–4, no. 2 (2002–2004).

Conference Proceedings

The proceedings of the congress *Nikolaus Cusanus zwischen Deutschland und Italien. Beiträge eines deutsch-italienischen Symposiums in der Villa Vigoni, 28. März bis 1. April 2001*, ed. M. Thurner (Berlin, 2002), provide a good insight into the status of Cusanus research at the beginning of the third millennium. This publication appeared on the occasion of the Jubilee Year 2001. Another is *Nikolaus von Kues 1401–2001. Akten des Symposiums in Bernkastel-Kues vom 23. bis 26. Mai 2001*, ed. K. Kremer and K. Reinhardt, *MFCG* 28 (2003). Also *Coincidência dos opostos e concórdia: Caminhos do pensamento em Nicolau de Cusa. Actas do Congresso Internacional realizado em Coimbra e Salamanca nos dias 5 a 9 de Novembro de 2001*, ed. J. M. André and M. Álvarez Gómez (Coimbra, 2002); *Coincidencia de Opuestos y Concordia: Los Caminos del Pensamiento en Nicolás de Cusa. Actas del Congreso Internacional celebrado en Coimbra y Salamanca los dias 5 a 9 de Noviembre de 2001* 2, ed. M. Álvarez Gómez and J. M. André (Salamanca, 2002). In addition, *Nicholas of Cusa: A Medieval Thinker for the Modern Age*, papers given at a congress held at Waseda University, Tokyo, October 6–8, 2000, ed. K. Yamaki (Richmond, Surrey, 2002).

Exhibit Catalogs

Three exhibit catalogs, each richly illustrated, appeared in connection with the Cusanus Jubilee with the general title, *Circa 1500. Landesausstellung 2000*: first, *"Leonhard und Paolo. Ein ungleiches Paar"* (Lienz, Bruck Castle); second, *De ludo globi: Vom Spiel der Welt* (Brixen, Brixen Castle); and third, *An der Grenze des Reiches* (Besenello, Beseno Castle), all published in Milan, 2000; material on NC and *De ludo globi*, 352–420. The same in Italian: *Circa 1500. Mostra storica 2000; De ludo globi*; and *Il gioco del mondo* (Bressanone), again published in Milan, 2000. In addition, *Nikolaus von Kues in seiner Welt. Eine Ausstellung zur 600. Wiederkehr seines Geburtstages*, a catalog for the exhibit in the Episcopal Cathedral and Diocesan Museum of Trier and in the St. Nicholas Hospital in Bernkastel-Kues, May 19 to September 30, 2001, designed by Marc-Aeilko Aris (Trier, n.d. [2001]). The catalog includes a variety of authors.

Recent Introductions to Cusanus

A variety of authors present a broad array of Cusanus's thought in *Introducing Nicholas of Cusa: A Guide to a Renaissance Man*, ed. C. M. Bellitto, T. M. Izbicki, and G. Christianson (New York, 2004). The volume includes a bibliography and a "Brief Glossary of Cusan Terms" (see also "Bibliographies" previously). Three shorter introductions are M. de Gandillac, *Nicolas de Cues*, with annotated excerpts from his writings (Paris, 2001); K. Kremer, *Nicholas of Cusa, 1401–1464: One of the Greatest Germans of the Fifteenth Century* (Trier, 1999), trans. F. and H.-J. Kann (Trier, 2002); and K. Flasch, *Nikolaus von Kues in seiner Zeit: Ein Essay* (Stuttgart, 2004).

Examining Cusanus's Philosophy

Highly regarded but also strongly criticized for its radically genetic point of view and method of interpretation is K. Flasch, *Nikolaus von Kues. Geschichte einer Entwicklung. Vorlesungen zur Einführung in seine Philosophie* (Frankfurt am Main, 1998). Another, containing an interpretation of the most important philosophical writings, is C. L. Miller, *Reading Cusanus. Metaphor and Dialectic in a Conjectural Universe*, in *Studies in Philosophy and the History of Philosophy 37* (Washington, D.C., 2003).

Ethics

D. J. De Leonardis, *Ethical Implications of Unity and the Divine in Nicholas of Cusa*, in *Cultural Heritage and Contemporary Change*, Series 1, *Culture and Values* 10 (Washington, D.C., 1998). Numerous aspects of the subject also appear in *Sein und Sollen: Die Ethik des Nikolaus von Kues*, *MFCG* 26 (2000).

History of Cusanus's Reception

S. Meier-Oeser draws a revised picture of Nicholas of Cusa's influence on philosophy in *Die Präsenz des Vergessenen. Zur Rezeption der Philosophie des Nicolaus Cusanus vom 15. bis zum 18. Jahrhundert*, in *Buchreihe der Cusanus-Gesellschaft (BCG)* 10 (Münster, 1989). The volume contains valuable bibliographical references to literature before 1847. Also H. Benz, *Individualität und Subjektivität: Interpretationstendenzen in der Cusanus-Forschung und das Selbstverständnis des NvK, BCG* 13 (Münster, 1999).

Theology and Spirituality

P. J. Casarella, *Nicholas of Cusa's Theology of the Word*, Ph.D. diss. (Yale University, 1992). Also M. Thurner, *Gott als das offenbare Geheimnis nach NvK* (Berlin, 2001).

Christology

A. Kaiser, *Möglichkeiten und Grenzen einer Christologie "von unten." Der christologische Neuansatz "von unten" bei Piet Schoonenberg und dessen Weiterführung mit Blick auf NvK, BCG* 11 (Münster, 1992). Also numerous essays by K. Reinhardt, especially those in *MFCG*.

Mysticism

L. Dupré, "The Mystical Theology of Nicholas of Cusa's "De visione dei," in *Nicholas of Cusa on Christ and the Church* (see "Anthologies" following), 205–20. W. Beierwaltes, "Mystische Elemente im Denken des Cusanus," in *Deutsche Mystik im abendländischen Zusammenhang*, ed. W. Haug and W. Schneider-Lastin (Tübingen, 2000), 425–46. H. L. Bond, "Mystical Theology," in *Introducing Nicholas of Cusa* (see "Recent Introductions" previously), 205–31. W. J. Hoye, *Die mystische Theologie des Nicolaus Cusanus*, in *Forschungen zur europäischen Geistesgeschichte* 5 (Freiburg-Basel-Vienna, 2004).

Cusanus and the Modern Devotion

E. Meuthen, "Cusanus in Deventer," in *Concordia discors* (see "Anthologies" following), 39–54. N. Staubach, "Cusani laudes. NvK und die Devotio moderna im spätmittelalterlichen Reformdiskurs," in *Frühmittelalterliche Studien* 34 (Berlin, 2000): 259–337. J. F. M. Hoenen, "Ut pia testatoris voluntas observetur. Die Entstehung der Bursa Cusana zu Deventer," in *Conflict and Reconciliation: Perspectives on*

Nicholas of Cusa, ed. I. Bocken, *Brill's Studies in Intellectual History* 126 (Leiden, 2004): 53–73.

Ecumenism and Peace among Religions

Among others, B. Helander, *Nicolaus Cusanus als Wegbereiter auch der heutigen Ökumene*, in *Acta Universitatis Upsaliensis* 3 (Uppsala, 1993); W. A. Euler, *Unitas et Pax. Religionsvergleich bei Raimundus Lullus and NvK* in *Religionswissenschaftliche Studien* 15 (Würzburg-Altenberge, 1995); G. Wenz, "De pace fidei. NvK als Theoretiker eines christlichen Ökumenismus," in Nikolaus von Kues 1401–2001," *MFCG* 28 (2003): 189–209.

Mathematics, Including Its Speculative Function

L. de Bernart, *Cusano e i matematici*, in *Pubblicazioni della Classe di Lettere e Filosofia Scuola Normale Superiore* 20 (Pisa, 1999). J.-M. Counet, *Mathématiques et dialectique chez Nicolas de Cuse*, in *Études de philosophie médiévale* 80 (Paris, 2000). J.-M. Nicolle, *Mathématiques et métaphysique dans l'œvre de Nicolas de Cues* (Villeneuve d'Ascq, 2001), with French translation of the mathematical writings.

Anthologies, *Festschriften*

The following are a few of the numerous anthologies and *Festschriften* with recent contributions to Cusanus research.

Anthologies include G. von Bredow, *Im Gespräch mit NvK. Gesammelte Aufsätze 1948–1993*, ed. H. Schnarr, in *BCG, Sonderbeitrag zur Philosophie des Cusanus* (Münster, 1995). F. E. Cranz, *Nicholas of Cusa and the Renaissance*, ed. T. M. Izbicki and G. Christianson, in *Variorum Collected Studies Series*, CS 654 (Aldershot, 2000). H. G. Senger, *Ludus sapientiae. Studien zum Werk und zur Wirkungsgeschichte des NvK*, in *Studien und Texte zur Geistesgeschichte des Mittelalters* 78 (Leiden-Boston-Cologne, 2002). K. Kremer, *Praegustatio naturalis sapientiae. Gott suchen mit NvK*, in *BCG, Sonderbeitrag zur Philosophie des Cusanus* (Münster, 2004).

Festschriften include *Nicholas of Cusa in Search of God and Wisdom: Essays in Honor of M. Watanabe by the American Cusanus Society*, ed. G. Christianson and T. M. Izbicki in *Studies in the History of Christian*

Thought 45 (Leiden-Boston-Cologne 1991). *EN KAI ΠΛΗΘΟΣ. Einheit und Vielheit. Festschrift für K. Bormann zum 65. Geburtstag,* ed. L. Hagemann and R. Glei, in *Religionswissenschaftliche Studien* 30 (Würzburg-Altenberge, 1993). *Concordia discors. Studi su Niccolò Cusano e l'umanesimo europeo,* ed. G. Santinello, assisted by G. Piaia, in *Medioevo e umanesimo* 84 (Padua, 1993). *Nicholas of Cusa on Christ and the Church: Essays in Memory of Chandler McCuskey Brooks for the American Cusanus Society,* ed. G. Christianson and T. M. Izbicki, in *Studies in the History of Christian Thought* 71 (Leiden-Boston-Cologne, 1996). *Nicholas of Cusa and His Age: Intellect and Spirituality. Essays Dedicated to the Memory of F. E. Cranz, T. P. McTighe and C. Trinkaus,* ed. T. M. Izbicki and C. M. Bellitto, in *Studies in the History of Christian Thought* 105 (Leiden-Boston-Cologne, 2002).

Index

Nicholas of Cusa: A Sketch for a Biography was designed and typeset in Dante by Kachergis Book Design of Pittsboro, North Carolina. It was printed on 55-pound Natural and bound by Versa Press of East Peoria, Illinois.